The Multinational Corporation,
The Nation State and the Trade Unions:
An European Perspective

The Multinational Corporation, The Nation State and The Trade Unions: An European Perspective

by

GUNNAR HEDLUND

and

LARS OTTERBECK

Stockholm School of Economics
Institute of International Business

The Comparative Administration Research Institute

Distributed by the Kent State University Press

Copyright © 1977 by
The Comparative Administration Research Institute
Kent State University
All rights reserved
ISBN: 0—87338—198—X
Library of Congress Cataloging in Publication Data
Library of Congress Catalog Card Number: 76—42447
Main entry under title:

Hedlund, Gunnar and Otterbeck, Lars

The multinational corporation, the nation state and
the trade unions—an European perspective.

Ohio   Kent State University Press
1977   9—23—76

First Printing

Published by the
Comparative Administration Research Institute,
Kent State University
Kent, Ohio 44242

Photosetting by Thomson Press (India) Limited, New Delhi

FOREWORD

This is a report on a field study of the attitudes and expectations of over one hundred people about the future. All the people interviewed occupy influential positions in Swedish society. The field work was carried out between November 1972 and May 1974. Parallel studies were taking place in the United States and—later—in Finland.

The report was first published in Swedish only, for two reasons. First, we felt that much of the material would perhaps be interesting only to Swedish readers. Secondly, a joint report was being planned with the research groups in the various countries where similar projects were being carried out.

We have now decided, however, to publish a somewhat condensed English version. So much spontaneous interest has been shown in our work internationally that such a version seems called for. Moreover, it has not proved possible to make all the comparisons between the different national projects that had been planned.

We also feel that the methods we have used to reveal people's attitudes, preferences and expectations with regard to difficult, complex and sensitive issues could be of interest to other scientists and could provide grounds for fruitful discussion. These methods are based on the theories of Russel Ackoff, Fred Emery, Hasan Ozbekhan, Howard V. Perlmutter and Eric Trist.

As regards the subject of this book—future relations between multinational corporations (MNCs), trade unions and the nation state—Sweden provides a fascinating arena for study. With 25 percent of its GNP in foreign trade, with a higher share of foreign investment per capita than the United States (e.g., 290,000 people employed by Swedish industry abroad compared with 930,000 at home in 1975), and with about 100,000 people working in foreign-controlled firms based in Sweden, the country should provide an interesting place for surveying attitudes to the MNCs. Also, Sweden's high material standard of living, its tradition of good labor-management relations, and its long period of social democratic government make it a country where enlightened views on the MNC "problematique" might be expected to flourish.

Indeed, as Professor Howard V. Perlmutter concludes in his postscript to this book, ". . . the big nations, like the USA, in some heroic insight may look to the smaller nations as models for the future."

This book is the result of several interacting group projects. We would like to thank all those—people and institutions—who have contributed to the realization of the various research projects upon which the book is based and who have helped in the development of the conceptual, theoretical and methodological bases of the work.

Howard V. Perlmutter, professor at the Wharton School, University of Pennsylvania initiated the discussions that led to the project, and has strongly influenced the research design and the theoretical framework of the study. He was engaged as visiting professor at the Stockholm School of Economics in 1972–73 and he has followed our project from its beginning to its completion. His support and advice have been invaluable assets, both from the scientific and personal point of view.

The researchers conducting the sister study in the United States took part in the consultative system, which has been of much importance to this international research process. Franklin R. Root and Bernard Mennis have participated in a very constructive way in these talks.

Professor Eric Trist and Professor Hasan Ozbekhan, also at the Wharton School, have influenced the study through the many long and interesting discussions we have had together, and through their writings. Trist has particularly influenced the methods we have used in the field research and Ozbekhan the way we have analysed the material. Their theoretical work has also been of great help to us in structuring our thoughts about the internationalization process.

Folke Kristensson, professor at the Stockholm School of Economics, has been scientific adviser to the project and has been a constant source of inspiration.

Among others in the world of academia who in various ways and at difficult stages have made a constructive contribution to the research process, we would particularly like to mention: J. Scott Armstrong, Curt Berg, Bengt Brodin, Bertil Kusoffsky, James C. Leontiades, Håkan Lindhoff, Sven-Erik Sjöstrand, Åke Sparring, Bertil Thorngren and Richard Wathen.

The project has been discussed at many seminars and conferences. In particular we should mention, and would like to thank, the participants at the following: 'Recent Research on the Multinational Firm,' arranged in Paris by the European Institute for Advanced Studies in Management in December, 1973; "Seminar on 'Futures of Sweden,'" arranged in Berlin by the International Institute of Management in January, 1974; seminars at the Universities of Stockholm, Uppsala and Lund, and at the Technical Institutes in Stockholm and Lund.

Since the publication of the Swedish version, we have had the pleasure of presenting our findings to a great many audiences, and have as a result been encouraged to go ahead with a translation. In particular, mention should be made of our presentations to the Brookings Institution, to the Social Systems Sciences Department at the University of Pennsylvania and to several groups of top management people at the Swedish Institute of Management.

As we all know, more is needed to bring a book into being than the various types of intellectual efforts mentioned above. The Swedish Institute of Management believed in the idea of this project at an early stage; the Institute engaged Howard V. Perlmutter and provided the financial resources required for the project. The Institute itself, and its director, Per-Jonas Eliaeson, have given us invaluable support throughout, and have provided the administrative resources required by a task of this size. Vanja Ekberg,

Britta Eneroth, Margareta Keijser, Barbro Orrung, Mona Söderman, Gertrud Wollin and Eva Åberg have all helped in making our thoughts communicable to others. Nancy Adler helped us translate our Swedish manuscript.

During the later stages of the project, financial support was also provided by the Bank of Sweden Tercentenary Fund and the Swedish Council for Social Science Research. The Economic Research Institute at the Stockholm School of Economics lent us the premises and administrative resources for carrying out this part of the project.

The help of all those we have mentioned here, and of many others as well, is hereby gratefully acknowledged.

Gunnar Hedlund
Lars Otterbeck
Stockholm, June 1976

CONTENTS

Introduction:
The Multinational Corporation,
The Nation State and the Trade Unions:
An European Perspective

It has been claimed that the multinational corporations, among other things, increase world welfare, are a threat to democracy, transfer technology to developing countries, exploit developing countries, undermine the trade union movement, speculate in foreign currencies, produce inflation, pay better wages than national companies, meddle in the politics of the host countries, etc.

This book discusses the issues that arise in connection with the internationalization of business. The book originated in a research project that was being carried out at the Swedish Institute of Management and the Stockholm School of Economics during the period 1972 to 1974. The project was called "Futures of Sweden in a Global Industrial System" and was one of several similar studies being made in various countries. The initiator of the studies was Howard V. Perlmutter, who was leading the Multinational Enterprise—Public Policy project at the Wharton School in 1972. The Swedish study was started in 1972; Finnish and Canadian studies began in 1973.

The purpose of all the studies was to try to discover and reach some understanding of the possible future shape of an industrial system that is becoming increasingly global. The relationship between MNCs, governments and trade unions was seen as crucial in the futures-creation process, and they represented the focus of the empirical research. This book presents and discusses the Swedish study. The Wharton study is reported in Perlmutter, Root & Plante (1973), and Root (1974). No report on the Finnish study is yet available in English.

BASIC POINT OF VIEW

The point of view adopted in this book is that the internationalization of business should be looked upon as a systemic process, no one part of which can be considered separately from all the others. The focus is thus not on specific issues such as the implications of the MNCs for employment, the possible evasion of taxation in MNCs, the effects on the efficacy of strikes as a way of negotiating wage deals for trade unions and so on. Instead, all these issues, together with many others, are seen as constituting a "mess," or a "problematique," as it has been called by R. A. Ackoff and Hasan Ozbekhan respectively. The ultimate purpose of the study is to help to develop improved methods for intervening in this complex situation, e.g., better methods for *planning*.

To accomplish this aim, it is necessary to reach some understanding of how the organizations and the people who affect the internationalization process act and interact in jointly creating the future. The (multinational) corporations, the organizations of the political system and the trade unions are the kind of organizations most likely to harbor these individuals.

PURPOSES

To attain the primary normative aim of the study, we formulated three specific subgoals of a more descriptive nature:

1. to identify future areas of conflict and cooperation between corporations, political organs and trade unions
2. to identify the perceptions of leading officials in corporations, political organs and trade unions regarding possible and desirable alternative futures
3. to analyse differences and similarities in these respects between Sweden and other countries, and thus to identify possible future advantages that Sweden may enjoy in comparison with other countries.

METHOD

Interviews were held with 108 top officials from the three systems studied. The respondents were asked about their expectations and plans with respect to the future. They were also confronted with alternative scenarios of the future. These had been constructed by the researchers and served several purposes: they provided a tool for the validation of other data, they supplied a basis for speculating in terms of forecasts contingent on developments such as those depicted in the scenarios, and they helped to enrich and enliven discussion of the interviews. An important part of the study was to feed information obtained at earlier interviews to the respondent in question, and thereby to encourage a dialogue about Sweden's policy for shaping and adapting to a future global industrial system.

STRUCTURE OF THE BOOK

Chapter 1 contains a short summary of the development of international trade and investment, together with a brief discussion of some of the more frequently debated issues that the internationalization of business has provoked. The reader who is already familiar with the subject matter can omit this purely descriptive chapter without jeopardizing his understanding of later chapters.

Chapter 2 discusses some possible future lines of development for the global industrial system. The necessity is stressed of finding new ways of coping with the complex problems that accompany the internationalization of business. The chapter concludes with an outline of three possible futures for the global industrial system as regards the relationship between corporations, governments and trade unions.

Chapter 3 provides an account of the methods used in the empirical research and in the execution of the study.

Chapters 4–6 present the results from the three stages in the study: at the company level, at the trade union level, and at the political level.

In Chapter 7, the results as reported in Chapters 4–6 are discussed in relation to one another. Some strategies for companies, trade unions and politicians are suggested.

The book concludes with a Postscript by Howard V. Perlmutter, which includes a comparison of the Swedish and the U.S. studies.

On the Internationalization of Industry: Some Facts, Some Impulses and Sweden's Role

In this chapter we will first provide a brief survey of what is known about the extent of international business and about the rate at which it has been growing in importance. These facts and figures can be found in almost any book on the subject and are included here simply to refresh the reader's memory.[1] Later in the chapter we will also say something about Sweden's relations with the multinational corporations, and mention some typical areas of conflict that arise between corporations and nation states.

WORLD TRADE

Since the end of the Second World War we have been witnessing a continual process of rapid internationalization in almost every sphere in the world economy. According to GATT, world exports at current prices have increased from 128 thousand million dollars to 413 thousand million dollars between 1960 and 1972; this represents an increase of 223 percent (Table 1:1).

A characteristic feature of the development of world trade has been that in many countries trade has grown more rapidly than production. Moreover, it is the trade of the industrial countries—and in particular their

Table 1:1

WORLD EXPORT 1960–1972
(Thousand Million Dollars, Current Prices)

	1960	1972		Increase 1960–1972	
	thousand million $	thousand million $	Share %	thousand million $	%
Total	128	413	100.0	285	223
Industrial countries	86	297	71.9	211	245
Developing countries	27	74	17.9	47	174
Eastern countries	15	42	10.2	27	180

Source: GATT trade statistics.

internal trade—which has grown the most. The industrial countries now account for over 70 percent of world trade; the comparative figure for the developing countries is barely 20 percent.[2] Further, the expansion of world trade has been concentrated to machines, means of transport, and chemical products, i.e. the same technology-intensive products that dominate the expansion within the different industrial countries. This expansion in world trade can be traced to the following factors, among others:

reduction in trade barriers

creation of trade blocs

development of world communications

rising incomes which have resulted in a rapidly increasing demand in many countries

greater specialization and multinational marketing.

This trend has not only produced an increase in trade but the internationalization of business enterprise itself, as manifest in the rapid growth of the multinational corporations, is perhaps the most important and most dynamic feature of postwar economic developments. This has occurred in an economic system which is based on the international division of labor and which allows goods, services and production factors to move between countries. Nonetheless, an important impetus to the internationalization of production has been the desire to overcome such trade barriers and other restrictions as have existed.

CONCENTRATION AND INTERNATIONALIZATION

The great corporations grow more quickly than their environments. And even if the difference in growth each year is not so remarkable, in the long run it is leading to a completely new structure in the world economy.

Table 1:2

SALES OF THE LARGEST COMPANIES, GNP, AND VALUE OF INDUSTRIAL PRODUCTION IN THE USA 1964–72 AND SWEDEN 1965–72.

Annual increase			
USA 1964–72		Sweden 1965–72	
Sales in the 500 largest companies	9.7%	Sales in the 200 largest companies	9.8%
GNP at current prices	7.8%	GNP at current prices	8.5%
Value of industrial production	6.6%	Value of industrial production	7.6%

Source: The Federation of Swedish Industries: de Multinationella i Sverige (Multinationals in Sweden), Stockholm, 1973, p. 4.

The Federation of Swedish Industries provides the following striking comparison between the USA and Sweden, despite the differences between the two countries and between the companies that operate there (Table 1:2).

According to the UN, the book value of foreign investments in the world was 108 billion dollars in 1967 and 165 billion dollars in 1971, an increase of 53 percent (Table 1:3). In 1971 the USA accounted for a good half of this amount. The next biggest foreign investor was Great Britain, with about 15 percent of the book value. Sweden, with its 2 percent, had as great a volume of foreign investment as the USA in proportion to its population. Roughly speaking US investments were divided about equally between Canada, Europe and the rest of the world. Sweden's went predominantly to Europe, and almost exclusively to the manufacturing industry. Both Great Britain and the USA directed a large proportion of their investments to the extractive industries.

In 1971 the total turnover of the multinational corporations (MNCs) outside their own countries was about 300 billion dollars, of which amount US corporations accounted for about 200 billion dollars and Swedish companies for about 3 billion dollars. We can compare this with the figures for world trade, which in 1971 amounted to about 325 billion dollars.

Table 1:3

MARKET ECONOMIES: FOREIGN INVESTMENTS (BOOK VALUE OF TOTAL STOCK) 1967, 1971. MILLION DOLLARS AND SHARE OF TOTAL

Country	1967		1971	
	million dollars	percentage	million dollars	percentage
USA	59,486	55.0	86,001	52.0
Great Britain	17,521	16.2	24,019	14.5
France	6,000	5.5	9,540	5.8
West Germany	3,015	2.8	7,276	4.4
Switzerland	4,250	3.9	6,760	4.1
Canada	3,728	3.4	5,930	3.6
Japan	1,458	1.3	4,480	2.7
Holland	2,250	2.1	3,580	2.2
Sweden	1,514	1.4	3,450	2.1
Italy	2,110	1.9	3,350	2.0
Belgium	2,040	1.9	3,250	2.0
Australia	380	0.4	610	0.4
Portugal	200	0.2	320	0.2
Denmark	190	0.2	310	0.2
Norway	60	0.1	90	0.1
Austria	30	0.0	40	0.0
Other	4,000	3.7	6,000	3.6
Total	108,200	100.0	165,000	100.0

From "Multinational Corporation in World Development," UN, 1973.

Table 1:4

A VERY ROUGH ESTIMATE OF THE NUMBER OF FOREIGN EMPLOYEES IN 1972. DIVIDED ACCORDING TO THE COMPANIES' COUNTRY OF ORIGIN

USA	4,500,000	The Netherlands	400,000
Great Britain	1,200,000	Canada	300,000
Switzerland	400,000	Japan	250,000
West Germany	400,000	Sweden	240,000

Source: The Federation of Swedish Industries: de Multinationella i Sverige, (Multinationals in Sweden), p. 5.

The number of employees in the foreign subsidiaries of the multinational corporations has been estimated at around eight million people (Table 1:4).

To these figures we have to add the workforce in the respective companies own countries. In Swedish companies the proportion of foreign employees is often very high—for the 50 largest foreign investors it is almost 40 percent. If we allow for a somewhat lower proportion (about 30 percent) for the US companies, in particular, we can roughly assess the total number of employees in MNCs throughout the world at about 25 million. In comparison, employment in industry in the OECD countries in 1970 amounted to slightly over 100 million people.

In 1968 a third of the book value of foreign investments was to be found in the developing countries, but these investments corresponded to a sixth of world production and a fifth of world trade only (if the centrally planned economies are not included).[3] The dominating position of the USA can be seen from the fact that its total investments in EEC are 3.5 times greater than EEC's in the USA, 7 times greater than Canada's and 70 times greater than those of Latin America.[4]

Although the USA dominates clearly in absolute terms, it does not do so in terms of growth. In many markets, Japan and various European countries have made considerable inroads.

We can also note that the foreign investments of several industrial countries have a positive effect on the balance of payments of the home country. The USA's direct net investment flow per year in 1970 was 4.4 billion dollars. Net returns (remittancies, royalties and fees minus outflow of investment capital) averaged 7.2 billion dollars per year during 1966–70. Sweden, too, experienced a positive contribution to the balance of payments during this period. Net returns amounted to about 28 million dollars per year.[5] Countries with a negative balance were, to mention the largest deficits, West Germany, Canada, Australia and South Africa.[6]

WHY COMPANIES INVEST ABROAD

The basic argument in favor of foreign investment from the company's point of view is long-term profitability. In choosing between countries, a company might consider such things as growth prospects, the country's general attitude towards foreign investment and expectations regarding future economic policy. Another important impetus behind the choice between exports and local production is the need to get inside the buying countries' tariffs and other barriers to trade.

The theory of international trade and investment provides several theoretical approaches to this problem. The following extract from an article published in English by one of the authors of the present book can serve to illustrate this.[7]

Theory of Factor Proportions

The first names we encounter in a review of such theories are those of Heckscher and Ohlin. Their theory of factor proportions, first formulated by Ohlin more than 50 years ago, has proved to be more durable in explaining the phenomenon than most theories. The best known, and very simplified, version of the factor proportion theorem says that relatively good supply of capital in a country leads to exports of capital intensive production. To put it more generally, a country tends to export the goods for which its availability of resources is suitable.

Translated into terms of localization theories, the Heckscher-Ohlin theorem means that, in an international exchange of goods, the goods are produced where production conditions are most favorable. If we shift our level of analysis from nation to company, and move to a different period of time from that in which the factor proportion theory was formulated, the following line of reasoning can be set up A multinational company tends to divide its activities throughout the world in such a way that it takes advantage of the differences between countries in terms of availability of capital or labor, so that capital-intensive production is carried out in countries which offer good availability of capital and labor-intensive production is carried out in countries which have ample supplies of labor. If prices of various factors of production reflect their scarcity, which in general is an acceptable approximation in a market economy, such a division of a multinational company's activities should in principle be completely compatible with the desire to produce at the lowest possible cost. This assumes that the costs of coordination and integration will not exceed the profits which can be made through dividing activities according to the theory of factor proportions.

Economies of Scale

Another theory, to which Ohlin also contributed, along with—among others—the Belgian Drèze and the American Hufbauer, takes as its starting point the degree of economy of scale. A large domestic market encourages the production of items where the advantages of scale are large. In countries with small domestic markets, production tends to be concentrated on goods whose manufacture does not offer any special advantages of scale. Multinational companies should thus, according to the theory, tend to adapt their production to the countries' domestic markets. In large countries, they should manufacture products offering advantages of scale, and in small countries products without any special advantages of scale.

If we look at a typical localization pattern of multinational companies, we find a very mixed picture. Typical mass production items, such as electronic components, are often produced in countries with small domestic markets, e.g. in the Philippines and Taiwan. On the other hand manufacturers in small, highly industrialized countries often produce goods that do not show any large economies of scale and sell them to the world market. To the extent that such manufacturers are parts of multinational companies, they are often in a conglomerate. Some examples are the U.S.-owned but Sweden-based companies Stenberg-Flygt and Sweda. On the other hand, the American automobile and steel industries and the chemical industries in most industrialized countries are examples that support the economies-of-scale argument.

'Human Skills'

A third theory stresses the labor force and its level of knowledge and education. Good availability of highly trained or skilled labor leads to an export of sophisticated products, while relatively good availability of unskilled labor leads to exports of products whose manufacture and marketing do not require any high level of skills. The best known supporter of this theory is Leontief, who in a famous paradox found that the U.S., the world's most capital-rich country, had a trade balance showing that the country's exports were more labor-intensive than its imports. This observation is not in line with the Heckscher-Ohlin theorem and an explanation can be sought in the composition of the labor force. The fact that the U.S. had a higher educational level than other countries was one conceivable explanation, in that the exports consisted of products requiring more educated labor.

The Theory of Product Life Cycles

We can finally mention a fourth theory, which has become increasingly well known in recent years. It is generally known as the Theory of Product Life Cycles. Well-known economists associated with it are Vernon and his colleagues Hirsch, Stobaugh and Wells. The theory was developed on the basis of earlier contributions by Burenstam Linder, Kravis and Hufbauer. Up to now, empirical studies have been carried out primarily on American companies and products. Very simplified, the argument is as follows:

American companies develop products based on the requirements of the domestic market. This domestic market is larger than any other market, and consumers there have a high living standard. Natural resources are also plentiful. Eventually, these new products and processes are introduced in countries other than the U.S. through exports. When exports are threatened by local manufacturing, American companies establish (or purchase) manufacturing subsidiaries in order to maintain whatever advantage they still have of having been first on the market. In this way, they can maintain the oligopolist's advantages for a time. Eventually, however, their position in the market for this product or process is weakened by increasing local competition.

The importance of international trade in the case of a particular product, and its connection with the product's life cycle, can be illustrated with the chart below. Studies which, on the whole, support this theory have been made for synthetic materials, electronics, office machines, consumer capital goods and Western movies. (Wells, 1972).

Studies of how the life cycle theory can be applied to (and must be modified for) European companies' products are under way. One complicating factor is that European companies are faced with a more complex choice of new markets. For an American company, it has always been true that activity abroad is in countries smaller and with lower living standards than the U.S., but for European companies, there is a much greater choice countries larger, of equal size, or smaller, with higher, equally high, or lower standards of living.

However, let us return to the life cycle theory and see how site selection affects the first stage of the life cycle. Up to now, we have assumed that the origin is in the U.S.

But if it is specifically American market or demand conditions that lead to the development of new products, we may ask why it should be only American companies that are first to begin manufacturing. Why shouldn't the first move be made by companies in Europe or Japan, where manufacturing costs are lower?

The explanation can be sought among the following factors. If, for example, the American defense establishment is the purchaser, which has often been the case for new products, processes and materials, a customary condition is that manufacturing take place in the U.S. For many products, there is not usually, at the beginning of the life cycle, any particularly strong

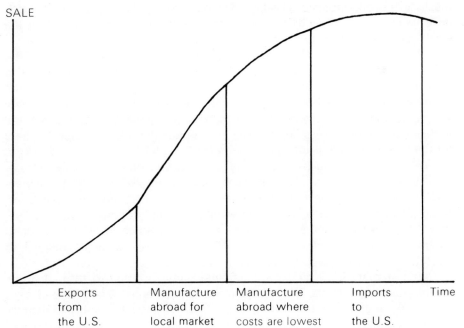

| Exports from the U.S. | Manufacture abroad for local market | Manufacture abroad where costs are lowest | Imports to the U.S. | Time |

The chart illustrates the probable connection between the life cycle of a product which is manufactured in the U.S. initially, and the localization of production as well as the direction of trade for this product.

reason to hold costs down. The determining factors at this point are not those connected with costs. The product is new, it has no direct substitute, the manufacturer has, during a short period, a monopoly position.

In addition, localization within the U.S. is favored by considerations of quick and varied communications needs within the company as well as between the company and its customers, suppliers, and consultants.[8]

This is part of the background to the location pattern of the multi-national corporations, as it is presented in foreign trade theory. It should be emphasized that, of the four theories presented, the first three—factor proportions, scale economy and human skills—were formulated to explain *trade between nations* before the spread of the multinational corporations was perceived as an important feature of the world's economy. The fourth theory was developed from empirical studies of American companies.

One more approach to the explanation of the impulses behind the foreign investment behavior of the MNCs is provided by the theory of oligopoly behavior.

Oligopoly—Mature or Undifferentiated

Let us take an industry with enormous advantages of scale, both in production and marketing. The major companies in the industry have long been multinational. The industry's technology is widespread and available to anyone. To be sure, it does cost something to acquire it, but the know-how is there. The knowledge also exists, although it is not as readily available, of raw material sources. A rigid price structure prevails on the market as a result of the oligopolistic situation. On occasion, short-term, largely local, price wars occur, either begun by a small new company or by one of the established companies temporarily experiencing overcapacity.

The major companies in this oligopolistic situation have as a goal the defense of their position. Large changes in the structure are not judged to be possible. The maintenance of a world market position requires the maintenance of a position in raw material sources, production and markets. The companies seek to protect price stability and always to be represented in their competitors' areas. In this way they reduce the risks (or opportunities) for unpleasant (or pleasant) surprises.

An example of such an industry is oil. Seven dominant companies— "the Seven Sisters"—all watch each other carefully and all participate in seeking new fields in Latin America, the Middle East, and offshore areas. None of them is eager to be unrepresented on any national market or any new raw-materials area, such as natural gas. And price levels are watched so that no dramatic changes occur. The economic resources needed to crush any troublesome competitor on a local market are available.

The stability for which the companies strive is attained through three means—signals, cartels, and cooperative agreements. A signal can take the following form: "I know that you intend to disturb me on Market X. If you don't leave me alone, I will get you on Market Y." Examples of this type of signal can, in a small perspective, be seen on the Swedish domestic fuel market.

Cartels take the form of more permanent signals, such as an agreement on how the market is to be divided up between the different parties. The cooperative agreement is a third way to assure stability. If two persons are in the same boat, both are interested in seeing that it stays afloat. It is difficult to throw one's fellow passenger overboard without winding up in the water oneself.

If a company becomes sufficiently large, it can also defend its own position, in addition to these three measures, through far-reaching vertical integration. We can see various examples of this, varying according to differences in technical conditions, legislation, and economic conditions. In the oil industry, for example, we can see that "the Seven Sisters" are integrated all the way from the raw material source to the gasoline pump and often even a bit further through expanding the assortment of goods sold at the stations. Keeping competition away through pricing policies that correspond to the demands of the amounts of capital and knowledge needed to enter the business at various stages is a tactic that oil companies are considered to use rather successfully. This tactic becomes less effective as the industry approaches the state of the "mature oligopoly," where, as indicated earlier, scale advantages are large and know-how is widespread.

The aluminium industry is an example where advantages of scale are enormous and the technology is rather esoteric. The copper industry's technology is more widespread, which can be seen in the relatively greater success that various nations have had in nationalizing the copper industry than they have had in nationalizing the aluminium industry.

Rules of Site Selection

If we examine, in particular, the site selection behavior of companies in mature oligopoly situations we find a number of rules that they appear to follow. These rules have been to some extent indicated in the general description of company behavior given above. Refined and simplified, they can be expressed as follows:

1.   See to it that you are represented on your competitors' markets! They will not be able to hurt you on one market without letting up somewhere else.
2.   Match the competitors' raw materials sources! Even if you don't know whether there is oil in the North Sea, you must go along if the others are searching there. Just think if they should make a gigantic discovery and you have no concession there!
3.   Avoid taking action on your own initiative that disturbs the balance! Be ready to discuss with your colleagues before you do anything dramatic!
4.   If a competitor should take some action independently, which upsets the balance, imitate him immediately! This is the typical oligopoly case taken from price theory—always follow a price reduction. Then make an agreement so that the whole industry can, all together, quietly and gradually raise prices again!

For anyone who studies company behavior in such an industry, the result ought to be the following. The companies avoid all dramatic shifts of raw materials sources. They will not abandon either Venezuela or the Middle East. The companies avoid seeking too energetically or too visibly new raw materials sources. Changes in the industry are extremely small when it comes to action from the established companies.

Larger changes are always initiated by new-comers who are met with customarily very effective, but almost invisible, efforts from the established companies to restore order. An obvious example is Occidental Oil, which willingly purchased oil from Libya several years ago at a price that was much higher than the seven large companies considered conceivable at that time.

The localization pattern in a mature oligopoly is thus very static. Market behavior of the established companies is on the whole directed toward maintaining the status quo: the maintenance of market shares, raw materials sources, production facilities, and relations. Nearly every innovation, either in the form of new raw materials sources, new products, new processes or new technologies is a threat to the established order. The strongly established companies can only lose in any new and different arrangement. Many of the heavy industries in today's world display characteristics similar to this situation. It is not only the oil and gasoline industry, where we have selected some examples, but to a certain extent also iron and steel, copper and aluminium.

There are few examples of the mature oligopoly in Swedish-owned industry. It is much more common in American-owned industry or in Great Britain. The mature oligopoly is probably not the most central point to study in an analysis of the localization patterns of Swedish-owned multi-national companies. On the other hand, it is of course interesting for us in connection with the general development of multinational companies or such companies' actions vis-à-vis Sweden.

New Product Oligopoly

A point of more immediate interest regarding Swedish companies is the differentiated oligopoly or the oligopoly based on new products (seen in a longer time perspective). For such industries, in which we can place most of the highly developed manufacturing sectors in Sweden, the product cycle theory fits well, with modifications made for the home country in question. We can reasonably include here automobiles, aircraft, computers, electronics, telecommunications, and a large part of the chemical industry.

A typical feature of the new-product-based oligopoly is a "market-centered" development activity. This does not necessarily mean that the companies are market-oriented in any modern, subtle sense. It only means that we can ascertain that new product development often occurs as a result of knowledge of the demands of the local market. The innovator lives somewhere and belongs to some country and his environment is primarily connected with some industry or professional group. The probability that he will discover or design a product or a process which suits his immediate surroundings is larger than that he will come upon something that can be used in a completely different context.

If we look at the automobile industry, for example, we see that innovations such as the automatic gear box came first in the U.S., as did air conditioning for automobiles. On the other hand, fuel-saving, efficient engines, improved suspensions and cars that take up less space came from Europe.

Many inventions in the forest industry have come from persons directly involved in this industry. In general, the U.S. has been ahead of Europe in innovations of a labor-saving character, while Europe has often been first in saving energy.

The localization aspect of this is that production will most probably be first localized in the place where the innovator is. The whole process tends thereafter to flow according to the pattern outlined above for the life cycle.

International Scanning

However, there is one reason why this theory has in certain cases lost some of its value in explaining or forecasting events. Companies which are already multinational and which have built up resources and organizations to scan the entire world are less bound to the innovator's home regarding the localization of new production. Nevertheless, it appears likely that even in these cases, production will at first tend to be placed in the inventor's home country. During the stage of product development, the need for rapid two-way communication between designers, manufacturers and the market or purchaser is so large that it heavily favors localization close to the market or purchaser, apart from the cost differences.

Eventually, however, production tends to be moved. Factors that make this so, aside from cost differences, can be alterations in demand-supply conditions, limited profitability or trade policies.

A change in conditions on the supply side can concern new raw materials sources, new materials, or new subcontractors, usually in connection with the fact that knowledge of the production process has become widely known or in certain cases simply that sources at the place where production started are exhausted.

Changes in demand conditions can include the spread of knowledge of the product and how it can be used. In a typical case, this knowledge is spread from highly developed to less developed countries and always in the beginning to those groups which are most susceptible to foreign influences, that is, the upper classes and businessmen. If the product is regarded as static and the development level of the countries dynamic, then it can be maintained that the product's level will be reached by more and more countries and that it will with time become obsolete in the countries where it has become established.

Finally, trade barriers require the adaptation by companies to the policies of one or several countries. This can involve the establishment of local production, either by the original manufacturer who previously imported the product, or by a local company. In either case, the local production *may* mean that the distribution of resources among countries has become less efficient than earlier, when the product was imported.

For companies that are not long established on the international market, site selection is probably influenced by their lack of information of market conditions and production conditions. These companies no doubt possess less well-developed information-gathering resources than they would have in a world of perfect information. Such a world can be a realistic point of discussion in two special cases. One would be where oligopolisitc competition does not function according to the theory but resembles more what is known as monopolistic competition. The other case can occur when technical conditions create such large differences between alternative sites that the search for the site with the lowest cost becomes intensified.

It also appears probable that multinational companies, which are large and well diversified geographically, behave differently from small local companies. A more effective department for gathering and processing information reduces the costs of scanning (at least the marginal costs) for the multinational companies in selecting a site.[9]

For Swedish industrial companies it seems that scale economies in research and development, production and marketing are important factors, as well as the demand for local production and local adaptation that is raised by foreign customers and governments. Following a modification of the ideas behind the product cycle theory cited above, we could say that Swedish companies have been forced to find larger markets than the Swedish market, to be able to achieve a volume of business that can guarantee long-term competitive power in product areas where big development costs and a decreasing average cost of production are characteristic features. In the case of certain companies we could even argue that the access to foreign markets has been a prerequisite of a competitive stance on the home market.[10]

For example, it is difficult to imagine that Sweden would have a competitive ball-bearing industry, automobile industry or telephone industry if SKF, Volvo, Saab-Scania and LM Ericsson were not established on foreign markets.

SWEDEN'S ROLE

Some Basic Facts about Sweden

In order to interpret our subsequent discussion and the results of the field study correctly, it is necessary to have some knowledge of Sweden as a country: its geography, its economy, its culture, etc. We have, therefore, summarized some basic facts about Sweden below, so that the reader who is unfamiliar with the country may be able to follow our reasoning. Most of the figures quoted below are taken from a booklet issued by Skandinaviska Enskilda Banken called "Basic Facts about Sweden 1975."

Sweden covers 175,000 square miles (475,000 km²), which is approximately the size of California, or twice the size of the United Kingdom. The language spoken is Swedish, which belongs to the group of languages known as the Nordic languages. It resembes Norwegian, Danish and Icelandic. Protestantism is the state religion, but church attendance, and other indicators of religious interest, suggest that Sweden is one of the most secularized countries in the Western world.

Sweden has developed (over the past 100 years) into one of the richest nations (on a per capita basis) in the world. It was one of the poorest countries in Europe at the end of the 19th century, and has undergone a period of very rapid transition from an agricultural to an industrial or post-industrial society.

Contrary to what is often believed, most industry—about 94 percent—is owned by private interests. On other measures, however, Sweden stands out as a country where government has a large influence over the economy and over social developments. Total government expenditure in the budget year 1974/75 was about 85 M Skr (about 34 percent of GDP).

Below are some important economic indicators, describing Sweden as it is today.

	1965	1970	1974
Population			
Total population at end of year, 1,000	7,772	8,081	8,177
Number of inhabitants per km^2	17	18	18
Gainfully employed	3,740	3,850	3,960
Percentage distribution by sector			
Agriculture, forestry, fishing	11,3	8,1	6,7
Mining and manufacturing	33,8	28,8	29,6
Construction	9,0	9,6	7,4
Trade	15,0	14,4	14,1
Transportation	7,1	6,9	6,8
Banking and Insurance	3,9	5,0	5,4
Public administration and other services	19,8	27,1	30,0

	1950	1970	1974
Labor market			
Unemployment among members of employment funds (%)	2,2	1,5	1,5
Number of working days lost due to labor disputes, 1,000	40	155	57
GDP, consumption, investment (current prices)			
GDP, market prices M Skr (Skr 4.30 = 1 US $)	32,040	168,900	247,150
per capita, Skr	4,550	20,870	30,225
Private consumption, M Skr	22,080	91,500	131,650
per capita, Skr	3,135	11,305	16,100
Public consumption, M Skr	4,195	37,500	57,620
Private investment excl. dwellings, M Skr	2,775	14,360	25,410
Public investment, incl. roads, schools, hospitals, defense etc., M Skr	1,610	14,445	17,085
Indicators of economic standard			
Passenger cars per 1,000 inhabitants	36	286	323
Telephones per 1,000 inhabitants	239	557	633
TV-sets per 1,000 inhabitants	—	310	348
Consumption of electricity, KWH per capita	2,270	7,100	8,460
Paper consumption, kg per capita	70	187	223
Foreign trade and balance of payments on current account, M Skr, current prices			
Exports, fob	5,725	35,150	70,280
Imports, cif	6,135	36,250	73,000
Balance of trade	− 410	− 1,100	− 2,720
Balance of services and transfers	580	− 470	− 1,775
Balance on current accounts	170	− 1,570	− 4,495
Gold and foreign exchange reserves	1,155	4,275	8,323

	1974			
	Exports		Imports	
	MSkr	%	MSkr	%
Foreign trade by groups of commodities				
Foodstuffs	1,682	2.4	4,651	6.5
Forest industry products	17,877	25.4	1,530	2.2
Mineral fuel and oil	944	1.3	12,602	17.4
Iron ore and concentrates	1,904	2.7	7	—
Iron and steel	5,888	8.4	4,360	6.1
Other metals and metal products	3,846	5.5	4,060	5.7
Machinery and instruments	16,666	23.7	13,948	19.3
Cars and car components	6,268	8.9	3,805	8.3
Ships and boats	3,525	5.0	2,727	3.8
Shoes and clothing	858	1.2	2,612	3.7
Residue	6,776	9.6	21,746	29.9
Foreign trade by countries				
EFTA	15,703	22.3	12,211	16.7
EEC	33,753	48.0	37,524	51.4
Eastern Europe	3,530	5.0	3,876	5.3
USA and Canada	4,748	6.7	5,072	6.4
Latin America	2,752	3.9	2,035	2.8
Other countries	9,905	14.1	12,132	16.6

Swedish Foreign Investments

Swedish companies have more than a quarter of a million employees abroad, while a hundred thousand people work in foreign-controlled companies in Sweden. Growth in Swedish-owned companies abroad and in foreign-owned companies in Sweden has been very marked in recent years, whether it be measured in terms of employment or in terms of sales.

In relation to the population of the country the international operations of Swedish companies are very extensive, although the largest export companies in the country are small in international terms. The companies which invest abroad are by and large the same companies which rank as the large exporters, and the proportion of intracompany transactions in foreign trade is increasing rapidly. The Swedish companies with the largest international operations are listed in Table 1:5, where their total turnover, their foreign invoicing (total invoicing to foreign customers) and the number of people they employ abroad are compared. The 25 largest Swedish companies in 1974 have been classified in the table on a basis of these figures, either as D (domestic-market company), E (export company) or I (international company). Companies with more than 40 percent of total sales in foreign invoicing have been classified as export companies. Those that have more than 40 percent of total employment abroad have been classified as international companies.

Production subsidiaries dominate noticeably with regard to number of employees, but the number of sales subsidiaries is rising sharply (Table 1:6).

Since the usual trend is for direct export to be succeeded by export through sales companies, which in turn is replaced by producing subsidiaries, we can assume that there will be a further acceleration in foreign production.

Table 1:5

THE 25 LARGEST INDUSTRIAL COMPANIES IN SWEDEN, 1974.*

		Turnover	Foreign invoicing	Number employed abroad	IED-Class
1.	Volvo (automobiles)	10,537	7,152(1)	9,661(8)	E
2.	Johnsonkoncernen (conglomerate)	9,944	3,833(6)	2,734(20)	D
3.	Statsföretag (government owned conglomerate)	8,062	4,880(4)	2,229(21)	E
4.	Asea (electric power)	6,916	3,191(7)	7,938(10)	E
5.	SKF (ballbearing, special steel)	6,900	6,315(2)	48,366(2)	I
6.	Saab-Scania (automobiles, aircraft, computers)	6,552	2,733(10)	3,805(12)	E
7.	L M Ericsson (telephones, electronics)	6,023	4,971(3)	49,550(1)	I
8.	Gränges (mining, steel)	5,550	2,406(13)	3,320(17)	E
9.	Electrolux (home appliances)	5,535	4,009(5)	40,483(3)	I
10.	Cementgjuteriet (building)	4,561	471(42)	+[1]	D
11.	Swedish Match (matches, conglomerate)	4,284	3,099(8)	26,750(4)	I
12.	Stora Kopparberg (pulp and paper)	3,601	1,798(15)	+	E
13.	Sandvik (steel)	3,383	2,934(9)	12,917(5)	I
14.	Alfa-Laval (machinery)	3,181	2,709(11)	11,258(7)	I
15.	Atlas Copco (machinery)	2,949	2,651(12)	11,729(6)	I
16.	SCA (pulp and paper)	2,669	1,864(14)	+	E
17.	Boliden (mining, chemicals)	2,616	1,210(19)	+	E
18.	Beijerinvest (conglomerate)	2,543	948(23)	+	D
19.	BPA (building)	2,507	116	+	D
20.	Uddeholm (pulp and paper)	2,266	1,430(16)	+	E
21.	SSSF (pulp and paper)	2,025	1,150(20)	+	E
22.	Euroc (building materials)	1,943	646(31)	2,913(19)	D
23.	MoDo (pulp and paper)	1,752	1,384(17)	+	E
24.	AGA (gas, welding, electronics)	1,694	1,144(21)	7,862(9)	I
25.	Kockum (shipyard, machinery)	1,664	1,084(22)	+	E

[1] A cross in the column "Numbers employed abroad" means that the company is not among the 25 biggest in this respect.

* Monetary data in million Swedish kronor (SKR 4.30 = 1 U.S. $) and rank in parenthesis.

Table 1:6

FOREIGN SUBSIDIARIES OF SWEDISH COMPANIES

	Number of companies			Number of employees		
	1965	1970	1974*	1965	1970	1974*
Sales subsidiaries	583	905	1,320	24,826	42,702	71,200
Production subsidiaries	329	423	480	147,807	182,649	219,700
Total	912	1,328	1,800	172,633	225,351	291,200

Source: B. Swedenborg, Den Svenska Industrins Investeringar i Utlandet (Swedish
Industry's Investments Abroad), Uppsala: IUI, 1973.
*The figures for 1974 are preliminary and based on a report by B. Swedenborg that
is not yet generally available. In "sales subsidiaries" for 1974, also "other subsidiaries" have been included.

The engineering companies dominate with regard to Swedish foreign
establishments, with 63 percent of those employed abroad. It will be
remembered that they also dominated the increase in world trade. In the
case of the distribution of these employees among recipient countries, there is
a certain correspondence between Sweden and world trade in general, in that
the role of the EEC countries is becoming increasingly important. In 1970
57 percent of the employees in Swedish-owned producing subsidiaries
abroad were working in the present EEC countries, while 20 percent were
working in the developing countries and 7 percent in North America.

Foreign Investments in Sweden
The foreign-controlled sector in Sweden is quite small in an international comparison (Table 1:7).
Between 1965 and 1970 a sharp increase could be noted in Sweden's
small (internationally speaking) foreign sector, both as regards employment
and turnover. The engineering industry dominates with 44 percent of the
employees, closely followed by the chemicals sector with 26 percent. The
largest owner country is the USA, but EEC is expanding rapidly. In 1970,
47 percent of those employed in foreign-owned businesses were employed in

Table 1:7

FOREIGN-OWNED COMPANIES' SHARE OF
INDUSTRY'S TOTAL TURNOVER

Canada (1969)	58.1%	SWEDEN (1970)	9.7%
Belgium (1968)	33.0%	Great Britain (1963)	9.1%
Australia (1970)	27.3%	Turkey (1968)	7.6%
West Germany (1970)	21.3%	Finland (1970)	7.0%
Netherlands (1971)	18.9%	Japan (1970)	3.0%

Source: Federation of Swedish Industries: de Multinationella i Sverige (Multinationals in Sweden), p. 13.

EEC-owned companies, as against 37 percent in USA-owned companies. The largest foreign employers were Philips, ITT and IBM.

Sweden in the Global Industrial System
      As we have seen from the above, Sweden and Swedish companies have economic relations with other countries which are extensive in relation to the size of the country's economy. Import and export amount to one quarter of the gross national product; one fourth of those employed in Swedish industry are located abroad, and one tenth of Sweden-based industries' turnover is controlled by foreign-owned companies. In the course of its industrialization, Sweden has chosen—or at least accepted—dependence on what we will refer to henceforth as the global industrial system. A high degree of specialization, the lack of certain raw materials, and a small domestic market have together led to this dependence, which seems to be accepted by businessmen, by politicians, and by most trade union leaders (Cf. Chapters 4–6 below), and is felt to be a necessary condition for the country's high material standard of living.

CONSEQUENCES OF INTERNATIONAL ENTERPRISE

      The internationalization of the world economy has thus progressed rapidly since the Second World War, particularly in the case of direct investment. The result of the growth of the multinationals has been to increase the concentration of ownership and power. The effects of this are subject to much controversy.
      According to classical foreign-trade theory, free trade and the free movement of factors of production together lead to the greatest possible welfare for the world as a whole. Various versions of this thesis are usually put forward as the main defence of multinational corporations. Because of their freedom of movement in production and trade, it is said, they operate at the lowest possible cost, and this benefits the world's consumers by providing a more effective system of production and distribution.
      It is also often claimed that by their very size the multinationals create opportunities for research and product development on a scale which would otherwise not be possible. This know-how is subsequently disseminated by the companies to many countries. However, the positive effects of the technological development of the multinationals have been questioned on various grounds. Admittedly, investments of a size which would not other-wise be possible have certainly been made, thanks to the ability of the multinationals to mobilize large capital resources and because of their access to big markets. On the other hand, the various national authorities have barely had any influence on either the direction or the use of this research. Studies have been made in Canada to investigate how far direct foreign investment has contributed to an increase in productivity, and the results are not unambiguously in favor of the multinationals.[11] As far as investments in the developing countries are concerned, there is also the question of whether the capital-intensive technology that is being developed in the industrialized world is really of much value to the developing countries,

considering their employment problem.[12] Further, as a result of their financial strength and technological knowledge, the multinational corporations can further the development of an oligopolistic or monopolistic trend in the world economy.

The effects of the multinationals on employment have dominated the debate in Sweden during recent years. It is not possible to make an unambiguous and reasonably certain statement about the effect that Sweden's foreign investments have had on employment in Sweden. The question to ask, of course, is what would have happened if the companies had *not* invested abroad. Would they then have expanded further within Sweden, or would they instead have rationalized their Swedish production with reductions in employment as a result; or would they have done nothing at all? We know nothing of this, and all we can say is that *most* Swedish industrial investment abroad appears to be motivated by a desire on the part of the exporting companies to gain control of foreign markets, to get round trade barriers, or to adapt to demands for local production. There are, however, exceptions to this "rule," for example the investments of textile and apparel companies in Portugal and Finland, which are chiefly motivated by the lower wages in these countries. We will not here try to penetrate the issue of whether there are any conclusions to be drawn from these motives as far as consequences for the Swedish economy is concerned.

It can, of course, also be claimed that even if the sum of the world's employment opportunities is not constant, there is no guarantee that it would increase if boundaries were closed. If one country began to impose restrictions on foreign investment, other countries would probably follow suit, and the country which started the process could easily become the target for retaliatory measures from other nations.

The trade unions are naturally interested in the employment aspect of the multinational corporations' activities. This is particularly noticeable in the USA, where several investigations of the problem have been undertaken although without any definite conclusions being reached.[13]

One direct threat to the activities of the trade unions is the ability of the MNCs to move their operations between countries in case of strikes. Here, as in so many other areas, the problem is—in the words of the Federa-

Table 1:8

DEGREE OF WORKER ORGANIZATION IN SOME EUROPEAN COUNTRIES AND IN THE USA

SWEDEN	70%	Luxembourg	35%
Belgium	55%	West Germany	30%
Denmark	50%	Ireland	30%
Austria	50%	Netherlands	30%
Great Britain	40%	Italy	20–30%
Norway	40%	Switzerland	25%
Finland	35%	USA	25%

Source: S. Hugh-Jones: "Trade Unions: The Weaker the Worse." *Vision*, 15 (February), 1971, p. 26. (From Levinson—Sandén, 1972, p. 112).

tion of Swedish Industries—that "the multinational corporations have been able to exploit the economic internationalization considerably more effectively than national governments and trade organizations".

Table 1:8 shows the different conditions for trade union activity in various countries. These differences allow the MNCs greater room for maneuvers.

The governments of the various countries also feel the consequences of being left behind in the internationalization process. In the area of taxation we know that by manipulating intracompany prices, by varying credit times on deliveries within the company, by pricing internal consultant services, by juggling with royalties and so on, companies have plenty of opportunities for showing their profits in the country which is the most favorable for them. Sweden has entered into double-taxation agreements with all its major trading partners, by means of which certain general rules have been created for the taxation of multinational corporations, but these rules cannot effectively prevent transfers of profits within the companies with the help of internal settlements. One cannot avoid a strong suspicion that the foreign oil companies in Sweden are conducting operations of this type, when one compares their reported profits with the profit reported by Swedish-owned OK (a consumers' cooperative with about one fifth of the petrol market), and with their profits in the low-tax countries.

The governments' problems are not limited to the taxation sphere. For many countries, in particular in the third world, one of the main problems is the effect on the balance of payments of income remittances to home countries. From the Swedish or the US point of view, this, of course, has the opposite impact, i.e. an improvement of the balance of payments. (balance of payments—in contrast to employment—is a zero-sum game.) Yet another problem that concerns the developing countries is the multinationals' potential or actual interference in national politics. We need only mention ITT and Chile to illustrate what can happen as a result of the MNCs' activities.[14] In the industrial countries the type of pressure of which ITT is accused is perhaps not as likely to occur. On the other hand, the governments of the industrial countries have to combat a level of inflation which has been blamed on the operations of the multinationals. According to the theories that have been put forward, the cash flow which is needed for the companies' new investments is positively affected by a rapid inflation, which gives the companies every reason to contribute to inflationary trends by an upwards adjustment of prices. To this we must add that the increasing tendency towards administered prices that accompanies the development of international oligopoly also contributes to inflation.[15]

It should be added here that most theorists in the field have greeted these notions with a certain scepticism. On the other hand, agreement is all the greater concerning the influence of the multinationals on world liquidity. The MNCs together have enormous liquid assets, which they can transfer relatively easily between countries. A great many of the adjustments in exchange rates which have had to be made in the last few years in Sweden and elsewhere may have been caused in part by private speculations against shaky currencies. This has come to represent a fundamental problem for

Table 1:9
PROS AND CONS OF
MULTINATIONAL CORPORATION FUNCTIONING

PRO	CON
1. Provide capital	1. Represent an expensive form of financing
2. Transfer technical know-how	2. Generate an outflow of capital
3. Educate the labor force	3. Concentrate on fulfilling and creating unnecessary needs and producing luxury products
4. Are highly efficient	4. Represent a state within (and above) the state
5. Generate exports	5. Demand privileges
6. Generate tax revenues	6. Absorb domestic capital
7. Create job opportunities	7. Underprice exports
8. Give better wages	8. Support the oligarchy
9. Reduce imports	9. Compete against domestic industry
	10. Create dependence

Source: S. Lindqvist, "Utsugning eller U-hjalp" (Exploitation or Aid), *Kommentar*, No. 2, 1970.

national economic policies, while it has also had a destabilizing effect on the world economy as a whole.

No account of the risks inherent in the growth of the multinational corporations would be complete without some mention of their role in the developing countries. No certain conclusions can be drawn; each person's view is ultimately strongly influenced by a variety of norms and values. Nevertheless it may be worth listing the arguments for and against foreign investment in the developing countries which generally dominate the debate on the subject (Table 1:9).

MEASURES AGAINST THE MULTINATIONAL CORPORATIONS

The multinational corporations beget problems for the nation states and for the trade unions. In recent years these problems have been the focus of attention in various quarters. Organizations such as OECD, the UN and the International Chamber of Commerce have launched comprehensive investigations, with a view to finding some kind of internationally acceptable rules of behavior for the operations of such companies. The UN has spoken of the need for a supranational deliberative body, where information about the multinationals could be collected and ventilated, and about establishing minimum requirements for the MNCs with regard to open accounting and information.

In the International Confederation of Free Trade Unions (ICFTU) and, earlier, in the International Metalworkers' Federation (IMF), similar demands have been on the agenda for some time. The importance of eliminating legal and other barriers to inter-state trade union solidarity has been emphasized, and demands have been raised for consumer and state participation on the boards of companies. Already in the 1950s the International Transport Workers' Federation (ITF) was pioneering for international standards in wages and working conditions for seamen employed on boats sailing under flags of convenience. Efforts in the same direction have been made in other trade union organizations notably among the chemical workers, and a certain amount of coordination of international action for solidarity has also been achieved, but a good deal remains to be done before the trade unions can operate as opponents on an equal footing with the multinational corporations.

In the nation states, too, legislation is being prepared to control international business activity. In Sweden controls on the foreign purchase of Swedish natural resources have been in operation since 1916. In spring 1973 the Swedish Riksdag passed a law giving the government greater powers to intervene in the foreign purchase of Swedish companies. Further-more, a special project group including the under-secretaries of seven of the departments most involved in international affairs and the vice president of the Riksbank (Sweden's central bank) has suggested that in considering applications for foreign investment permits, the Riksbank should no longer consider only the effect on the balance of payments, but also the effects of the foreign investment on Swedish industrial development and employment. A law to this effect was passed in 1974.

NOTES

1. For a more detailed account of data concerning the multinational corporations and interpretations of this data, the reader is referred for example to the following "Multinational Enterprises and Social Policy," an ILO publication on multinational enterprises. Geneva 1973. (*ILO studies and reports* N.S. 79). "Multinational Corporations in World Development." *United Nations Department of Economic and Social Affairs.* N.Y., 1973 (Henceforth referred to as the *UN Report*). Robock and K. Simmonds, *International Business and Multinational Enterprises.*

2. We are aware that the statistics presented in this chapter do not reflect recent changes in the world economy, such as the events following the oil embargo of 1973. For example, the share of world exports attributable to developing countries rose substantially in 1974 and has since declined again. The complexity of these changes calls for a far-reaching analysis which is beyond the scope of this book. Moreover, we are confident that the reader will bear these develop-ments in mind when interpreting the findings and conclusions of our study. Since most of the analysis was effected during 1973 and 1974, after the imposi-tion of the oil embargo, we also feel that our interpretation reflects more recent developments.

3. The Swedish Federation of Industries, *De Multinationella i Sverige.* Stockholm, 1973, p. 5.

4. *UN Report,* p. 18.

5. *UN Report,* p. 16.

6. *UN Report,* Table 20.

7. Otterbeck, L., "Multinational Companies and International Site Selection." *Skandinaviska Enskilda Banken Quarterly Review,* 3/1973.

8. *ibid.,* pp. 87–89.

9. *ibid.,* pp. 89–93.

10. Cf Kristensson, F., "Det Multinationella Företaget, Fackföreningen Och National-staten." *Internationella Studier,* 2/1973.

11. *See*, for example, *Foreign Ownership and the Structure of Canadian Industry*, Privy Council Office, Ottawa 1968, pp. 78–81.

12. *See* K. Levinson and P. Sanden, *Kapitalets International*, Lund: Prisma Publishers, 1972 and L. Pearson, *Partners in Development. Report of the Commission on International Development*, L. B. Pearson, chairman. N.Y.: Praeger Publishers, 1969.

13. *See*, for example, S. H. Ruttenberg, "Needed: A Constructive Foreign Trade Policy. Washington D.C.: AFL-CIO, 1971; *The Impact of US Foreign Direct Investment on US Employment and Trade; An Assessment of Critical and Legislative Proposals*. New York: National Foreign Trade Council, Inc., 1971; R. B. Stobaugh *et al., US Multinational Enterprises and the US Economy*, Boston: Harvard Business School, *mimeo*, 1972.

14. A. Sampson, *The Sovereign State of ITT*. N.Y.: Stein and Day, 1973.

15. Ch. Levinson, *Capital, Inflation and the Multinationals*. London: Allen & Unwin Publishers, 1971.

2

The Future of the Global
Industrial System

In the previous chapter we focused mainly on a description of the scope and nature of international business activity. It is our intention now to look at the whole question in a broader perspective. In particular we would like to develop and present some hypotheses about the possible futures of the multinational enterprises and their stakeholders.

The interest devoted by politicians, trade unions and journalists to the multinational corporations is accompanied by considerable disagreement as to the causes and the consequences of the development of these companies. Even among internationally experienced business executives the word "multinational" has a ring of something frightening and at the same time attractive. These men do not want their own companies to be encumbered with the label "multinational," even while they are busy planning for extensive foreign commitments.[1] And in the academic world there is noticeable uncertainty about how the multinational corporations should best be studied. The enormous complexity of the subject seems to make it impossible to fit it into the established academic organization. If we look at most of the research that has been carried out in the business administration field, we find that the main trend has been towards collecting material on the historically given behavior of companies, generally in order to alleviate, for coming generations of business leaders, the birth pangs involved in stepping out into international operations.[2] We also find that macro-economic research, apart from making detailed analyses of the structure of foreign trade, has frequently been concerned with the way in which ministers of finance should cope with the balance-of-payments problem generated by the activities of the MNCs, or with the effects these have on employment. At the same time some sociological and anthropological research is devoted to examining the cultural effects of MNCs on the countries in which they operate. This means that the study of the multinational corporations has generally started from some rather restricted point of view. We are convinced that the understanding of future events, and the ability to influence them, grows as the approach to the problems is given a broader base. The great variety of definitions of the concept of "multinational corporations" illustrates the kind of uncertainty that arises when we make the mistake of regarding a single aspect of some more complex whole as something which is interesting in itself.[3]

TOWARD A GLOBAL INDUSTRIAL SYSTEM

As we see it, the key to an understanding of the development towards an increasingly internationalized economy is to adopt a global view, and to regard the development of increasingly strong interdependencies between different parts of the world as the greatest change taking place in the global system.

Examples and expression of this interdependence are:

—rapidly increasing world trade—the creation of regional economic unions such as EEC, EFTA, LAFTA and COMECON

—environmental problems on an international level

—the formation of military pacts such as NATO and the Warsaw Pact

—increasing aid to developing countries

—global shortages of raw materials

—the establishment of international political or semi-political institutions such as the UN and OECD

—the emergence of companies with sales and production in many countries.

The list could be extended indefinitely, but the items we have mentioned are enough to illustrate our fundamental thesis: that decision-makers, wherever they may happen to live, must increasingly take into account in their decisions the effects their actions will have on events in other parts of the world and, conversely, that they are now influenced more than they used to be by what is happening in other parts of the world.

The driving-forces behind this trend lie in a variety of technological (and consequently economic) developments which, by expanding the transportation and communications networks, have made increasing industrial specialization possible. It should be remembered that even in a completely homogeneous environment there would still be room for regional specialization, if the advantages of scale were expected to compensate for the difficulties connected with transport, information flow, environmental change, etc.

Obviously technological development is not independent of the prevailing political and social conditions, and cannot thus be regarded as an autonomous process changing a passive world into something over which its inhabitants have no control. The social units—i.e., the people, groups of people and organizations—which shape and are shaped by the global system are many, and may be "institutionalized" to a greater or lesser extent. We might expect that the institutions which are "closest" to what we see as the fundamental impetus in the development towards increasing global interdependence, should also be the first to adapt their organizations and work forms to the new conditions. In Western market economies, business enterprise has been technology's major pioneer. Consequently, we have seen an increasing number of companies which have changed the structure of their production, financing and organization in order to exploit the opportunities and the demands associated with increasing international dependence to the full. We will not say anything more here about the theories and more technical considerations that lead companies to internationalize (discussed briefly in Chapter 1). The interested reader is referred to the relevant literature.[4]

Thus many companies have become multinational, while other organizations whose task has not hitherto been to concentrate on technical development—and which for legal and cultural reasons have been restricted to stakeholders in a single country—still retain their operations on a national level. In this sense, the multinational enterprises represent the "leading part" or leading system in the development towards increasing and more complicated interdependences between geographically distinct parts of the globe.[5]

Within this leading system the diversity of the leadership is considerable. Some companies or industries are both creators and users of technological developments; other companies, although multinational, have little connection with technological development at all. In the first group we find companies operating in electronics, communications technology and computer systems. The users of technology—for example, the tourist industry—occupy an intermediate position. Finally there are companies which build further on the colonial heritage, for example plantation estates. All these, however, can be said to represent parts of the leading system, since, in order to exploit their advantages in the global system, they help to increase interdependence.

For the planned economies of Eastern Europe, the situation appears to be a little different. Here it is the state authorities which administer technological progress. And the forces which lead Western companies to disseminate and exploit the blessings of technology throughout the world do not necessarily have the same relevance for a state (or for the officials of a state), which is normally guided by other considerations than those which motivate a company and its management. Ideological considerations are of great importance; purely nationalistic emotions may prevent progress towards increasing integration with the Western world; social consequences are generally evaluated by a state according to norms other than those applied by a company. However, it is dangerous to think of the state as a unit. If we look more closely, we can see that the state authorities embrace within themselves various groups of people who evaluate and react quite differently towards the change in the environment that technology has induced. The proportionately large number of engineers in the government organs of many East European countries suggests that there, too, an increasing industrial integration and specialization is regarded as something positive. In fact the idea is by no means alien to the communist states. One of COMECON's objectives, after all, is to establish a "socialist division of labor" by which available resources are exploited at maximum efficiency. Further, the East European bloc, as an industrialized and relatively rich part of the world, has the same interest as the Western bloc in ensuring for themselves the raw materials, the labor and the markets of the poorer countries in order to be able to maintain and increase their own domestic living standards, where growing demands for goods and services could not be satisfied within a closed economy. And current developments, too, support the hypothesis that the world, or at least the industrialized part of it, is approaching a state of international industrial interdependence that warrants the rubric *global industrial system*. And any reservations about the role of the Eastern bloc in this system will lose a good deal of weight when we look at the rapidly growing number of collaborative projects between private Western companies and East European states.[6] Economic return seems to carry more weight than ideological factors when the East European countries consider any strengthening of the bonds between different economic systems.

LEADING AND LAGGING SYSTEMS

The reader might conclude from the above that we see developments as predetermined, as something wholly decided by the "leading systems", i.e. mainly by privately owned Western companies and, to some extent, by the actions of the East European states. Let us, therefore, strongly emphasize that the term "leading" represents a *description of a historical development*: it does not constitute a legitimation of this development or a predetermination of the way the future will evolve. In other words "leading system" is not the same as "independent variable." We see the leading system as an open system influenced by other systems that also take part in the train of events that is *initiated* by the leading systems, and there is no a priori reason to assume that the latter are working for the same future as the former. However, many of the lagging groups will probably be less organized and less formally institutionalized, and will therefore probably find it difficult at least in the short run to assert themselves against the leading system. The consumers of the products of the multinational enterprises represent one such group. These people presumably have a considerable stake in future developments, but so far they have done little in the way of forming powerful organizations, and their understanding and assessment of the course of events is difficult to determine. Journalists, scientists, authors, children, etc. are all examples of such diffuse groups or clusters.

The power of the multinational enterprises is such that only some very strong and well established power groups in society could possibly switch the direction of the development for which the corporations are striving. Presumably it would also be necessary for these countervailing forces to be able to work at an international level, or at least that they should exist in fairly similar forms in many countries. Further, any claimants to the power at present commanded by the multinational enterprises must envisage a change in their own working conditions as a consequence of the internationalization of industry, if their efforts towards moulding the future are to switch events away from the direction that the leading system appears to intend. These considerations have led us to identify the *governments of the nation states* and other political bodies, and the *organizations of the wage-earners* in the various countries, as the most important components in the game for the future—a game in which the multinational enterprises are the leading players. This simple model of the state of the world during the coming ten years or so is illustrated in Figure 2:1 below.

Recent developments have been characterized by the growing contact networks established by the company system over and above national governments. This has altered the situation for the nationally organized stakeholder groups, of which the two mentioned in the figure are the most important in the sense that their actions have real implications for future developments. The leading actors in these lagging systems find themselves outflanked by the international corporations; they feel that the positions they have achieved within their own national borders are being threatened. At the same time they do have opportunities, both in their own countries and in

Figure 2:1

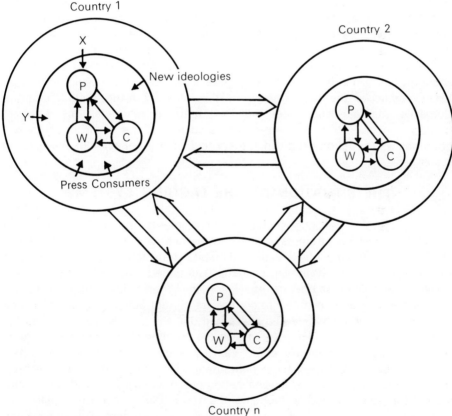

P = political organs
W = wage-earner organizations
C = companies

The arrows indicate the interaction between components in the system. To prevent the figure from becoming too unwieldy, the interactions between components in different countries have been combined in the thick arrows, which must not of course be interpreted to mean that the *countries* are acting as units.

collaboration with colleagues abroad, to establish defensive positions against the advances of the supra-entrepreneurial system. If we take a longer view, we can also envisage other groupings and other institutions in this role. We will discuss this matter further in Chapter 7.

One assumption on which the model in Figure 2:1 is based—and thus the arguments that we later derive from the model—is that each of the three systems is homogeneous internationally speaking. But, is it really reasonable to regard the Swedish government as sitting in the same boat as the government of the USA? Or to assume that the German and Kenyan trade union movements have common interests? The answer to these questions appears to be no. But it has been shown that the rapid expansion of the international activities of business companies has brought what were originally quite dissimilar parts of the international trade union movement closer to one another. Likewise, international political institutions such as the United Nations and OECD have discussed the whole question of the control of multinational enterprise. At least as far as the Western world is concerned, we are probably justified in regarding the political system and the trade union system, each in its own way, as internationally unified forces. The countries which are already very dependent on the international economy and on other countries in general are also those which are most keenly aware of the problems, while the larger countries with enormous domestic markets and extensive raw material resources are not yet equally concerned. In this sense, we could regard the small industrialized countries as the leading part in the context of the behavior of the lagging systems.

THE SITUATION OF THE LAGGING SYSTEMS

Up to now the actions of both governments and trade unions have consisted of various attempts to adapt to the behavior of the leading system. OECD's code for the liberalization of capital transactions provides a good example of how the industrialized nations changed their policies to make it easier for companies to operate internationally. When it has seemed necessary to interfere, and perhaps to try to counteract current developments, measures have been introduced here and there without any overall guiding strategy. This period of inactivity, or reactivity, in the companies' environment is now being replaced by what we could call a proactive and interactive stage.[7] Thus, the parties affected by the internationalization of business are now trying to look upon the internationalization process as a whole and to consider ways of predicting and influencing the ensemble, rather than taking up postures ex post towards discrete elements in the process. This constitutes the reactive approach. In the interactive approach, on the other hand, the areas of contact between the company system and the political system, and between the company system and the trade union system, are extended. The classical liberal view of the state as a kind of orderly who clears up the possible damage done by companies in the grip of market forces draws a picture of a state that is essentially inactive and sometimes even reactive, and that should ideally have as little as possible to do with the business world. The interactive era calls for close and frequent contacts between different parts of society in a way that is incompatible with the principles of divided power that prevail in the true "liberal" world.

In a bounded national economy both politicians and trade union leaders enjoyed a relatively calm life. Their main job was to strengthen their own positions within the relevant organization and to strengthen the organization vis-à-vis other power groups in society. Arguments were presented and influence was exercised along lines appropriate to a divided nationalistic world which everyone expected was going to last for a long time to come. The internationalization of the major opponent (major, that is, from the trade union point of view) — i.e., the companies — changed this stable environment. As long as international commitments were not undertaken as substitutes for some equivalent domestic undertaking (examples could be exports, banana plantations, tin mines, etc.), the term "internationalization" meant very little. However, when it became clear that the operations of the international companies were no longer directed solely towards satisfying needs and interests in the home country, and when institutions began to emerge which had no proper homeland and which could *choose* between different countries as the seat of production, then the decision-makers in the homebound political and wage-earner associations found themselves in a situation which had somehow got out of hand. This revolutionary change has called in question the value of many long-established organizational patterns; politicians and trade union leaders are having to cope with an environment that is much more uncertain both for themselves and for the organizations they represent. Thus, in all probability there are going to be difficult problems of adjustment as the lagging systems start to transform themselves from within, to make their organizations more efficient. And there will be pressure from power groups within the systems, pressing for the creation of "equilibrium" by changing the structure of the multinational corporations rather than changing the structure of their own organizations.

In any case the immediate future is obviously going to involve big organizational changes in all the subsystems in Figure 1. Moreover, when it comes to taking action in the emerging global industrial system, experience from the past has little to offer in the way of guidance. Because of the sheer complexity and extent of international interdependence today, very few general principles, rules, or strategies can be found for any of the institutions included in our model. Thus not only are organizational forms in a state of flux; new patterns of behavior, new strategies and new policies will all presumably have to be subjected continually to a process of testing and retesting. We are on the verge of a societal learning process, in which complex institutions must learn how to handle and live with a continually changing and uncertain environment.[8]

The novelty of the situation in which the players in this game for the future of the global industrial system are involved, together with the complicating factor of the pressure for organizational change, makes any sort of prediction about future developments extremely difficult. It is not even possible to say exactly what problems the emergence of an internationalized industrial system will bring. The consequences are so many, the aspects so varied and the whole so intermingled in a vast causal network, that we prefer to speak not of a set of problems but of a "problematique" whose "solution" must lie in reorganization at a higher systems level.[9]

Instead of trying to predict the future of the global industrial system, we will outline some alternative scenarios, all of which we believe could be realized, at least as far as their main outlines are concerned.

MULTINATIONAL CORPORATIONS AND THE WORLD COMMUNITY—THE OPEN SOLUTION

Classical—or neoclassical—economic theory generally prescribes a passive attitude on the part of the nation states towards the actions of private enterprise. Any interference in the free play of the market forces is said to reduce efficiency and jeopardize a satisfactory allocation of resources. Since the Second World War this doctrine has provided the basis for international economic policy in the Western world. It constitutes a sharp deviation from the trade warfare of earlier periods when protectionism prevailed almost permanently. Institutions were established to help the market forces to operate, rather than to push them in any particular direction. The Bretton-Woods Agreement was a first step, followed by tariff reductions within the framework of GATT, attempts to standardize technical norms, the liberalization of capital movements, currency convertibility measures, and the emergence of international institutions such as OECD, UNCTAD and the World Bank. Thus, except during the last few years, the trend has been towards a liberal future. In some countries even the trade union movements have supported this line, if they have taken any interest at all in such matters. Sweden stands out as one of the most liberal examples. During the structural rationalizations of the 1950s and 1960s the Swedish Confederation of Trade Unions (LO) agreed that neither the state nor the trade union movement should try to stop companies from moving into expanding regions of the country or from growing more quickly there. Any problems that arose from this were to be solved by means of general economic policy combined with selective measures (grants for moving expenses, retraining aid, etc.) to support those who were hardest hit. Until very recently the same theory was being applied to the structural problems created by foreign trade, but lately in both Swedish and other trade union movements attitudes have moved away from this liberal view. The emergence of the multinational corporations is regarded as a new element, quite distinct from the sort of problem that was previously met by liberal economic measures. This situation, together with the fact that the majority of the world's trade union organizations have never supported policies such as free trade even on a national level means that the trade union system as a whole must be regarded as a force operating *against* the liberal future.

Two factors argue in favor of the open solution: one is that, according to the economic theory mentioned above, this solution leads to maximum efficiency; the other is the present power of the multinational corporations. In some countries the companies have such close links with the political system that it seems unnecessary to distinguish between the two, and since this applies to a great extent to the large countries, we may well wonder whether the smaller nations' fear of an international business system will find any counterpart in the set of rules and working conditions that will confront the multinational corporations. However, by the time internationalization has assumed such proportions that even in the larger nations it is felt to threaten the power of the established politicians in the state, the gap between the internationally and nationally organized systems will be so great that governments of *all* countries will be more prepared to present a united front.

In addition to in the small and internationally sensitive industrialized nations, we can expect to find opponents of the purely liberal open alternative among the less developed countries. For them this world represents little more than a continuation of the humiliating colonial era, embellished with some of the outward signs of independence.

The suspicion that greets the multinational corporations among the majority of the voters in the industrialized countries also suggests that liberal economic principles—which are already reeling under the shock of regional problems, environmental pollution, and the production of cultural trash—will appear more and more as the right of the strong to legitimate their existence rather than as scientific truths.[10]

One way out of the conflict between the philosophy of "the invisible hand" on the one hand and the fear of undermined power and awkward external effects on the other, could be to combine a basically positive attitude towards the multinational enterprises with the setting up of internationally accepted guidelines for their activities. The difficulty here would be that the leading system would always be one step ahead of the controlling forces. New technological or organizational advances could provide the large companies with powerful tools, against which the rest of society was not yet alerted. Moreover, it would probably not be possible to create effective controls without a geographical and cultural independence as great as that enjoyed by the multinational corporations themselves. If this condition were fulfilled, new wide-ranging changes would be introduced, which would radically alter the conditions of the multinationals. Unfortunately, however, previous experience of similar attempts on the part of international institutions to establish uniform and globally applicable rules and effective sanctions does not encourage much faith in this solution to the problems of international enterprise.

Thus it seems that the open solution is dependent on the extent to which the multinational corporations and their allies among the nation states—i.e. generally the larger of the host countries for foreign investment—can succeed in maintaining their power. Theoretical arguments geared to ideas of economic efficiency which may support the alternative carry less weight.

MULTINATIONAL CORPORATIONS AND THE WORLD COMMUNITY—THE CLOSED SOLUTION

Because it is difficult to envisage any overarching international solutions to the MNC "problematique," other alternatives more limited in content and geographical scope can be of interest. As we have mentioned, conditions at present are very different in different countries. We therefore have good reason to wonder whether the countries most affected by the internationalization of business enterprise, i.e. the small industrialized countries and most of the developing countries, will be prepared to wait for the major industrialized countries to be forced by developments into the same camp. The anxiety which colours the debate about the MNCs and the immediate strong reactions that greet every perceived attempt on the part of the corporations to abuse the power they enjoy, suggest a future in which the various countries act individually on a basis of their own problems and opportunities. The guarded attitude of the developing countries is a function of their fear of political and economic dependence on the multinational corporations and on the home countries of the corporations—a fear which was reinforced by ITT's collaboration in the attempt to prevent Allende's election as President of Chile in 1970.[11] Furthermore, many politicians in the developing countries feel an urgent need to create a national identity, to nurture a belief in their country's ability to govern its own fate, and any similarity with conditions in the colonial era is seen as an obstacle to the birth of a national spirit. Events of recent years have shown that the political color of the régimes concerned makes little difference. Even governments which profess their adherence to the private capitalist approach, many of the Arabian oil countries, for example, are imposing an increasing number of restrictions, including direct takeovers, on the activities of the foreign-owned companies. Sometimes, too, they try to incorporate the operations of multinational enterprise in the economic planning of their own country, occasionally with conflict between host and home country as a result. An example of the complicated pattern of coalition which can arise when a government actively plans the internationalization of a domestic economy was the controversy over the Argentinian government's exhortations to subsidiaries of US-owned automobile companies to export to Cuba, a country on which the American government had laid a trade embargo. In that case the USA had to give in to Argentina's demands.

In the industrialized Western world, possible motives for restricting the freedom of movement of the multinationals are of a different type. To begin with, the developing countries—apart from the oil states—are very rarely the home of international capital; they figure solely as recipients of foreign investment. The picture in the Western world is more diverse. Moreover, the political anxieties of the developing countries do not have the same relevance in the industrialized world. In most of the latter countries the idea of creating or maintaining a national profile would be, if anything, extremely inopportune. (Undeniably the various "back-to-the-land" movements have recently altered this situation somewhat, and they may have implications for the future, perhaps mainly by providing legitimation for measures undertaken for other reasons.) Instead attention in the industrial world is focused chiefly on more immediate matters, such as the effect on national employment, national currencies, and inflation. Traditional economic measures cannot operate with much precision when the supposedly controlled system (i.e., the companies) has much greater scope for its actions than the supposed controllers (i.e., the political decision-makers).

It is interesting to note that the perception of this shift in power, rather than any detailed analysis of the actual effects of the MNCs on the economy of the social structure, is what lies behind the appointment of many commissions to investigate—generally with extremely vague directives—the MNCs. This sort of doubt often leads to paralysis or to panic action. In such a situation sensitivity to the feelings of the general public may be the decisive factor behind political decisions about the corporations with international operations and in many countries the often widespread popularity of action against "foreigners" suggests that a trend towards economic nationalism and a world hostile to the multinationals is not altogether improbable.

Apart from the reactions that an economy in the process of rapid internationalization can arouse, some longer-run and more general factors also point towards the introverted, national, and possibly even nationalistic solution. We have already mentioned various signs that many people are reacting against the industrialized society and against the system of centralized "expert" decision-making. There is no doubt that the size, the power, and the inaccessibility of the MNCs make them an easy target for such defensive attitudes—attitudes *against* rather than *for* anything. The various institutions associated with this general movement usually lack any kind of consistent history or ideology and, therefore, they also lack continuity. It is this kind of short-term thinking with its focus on opportune problems that characterizes the closed solution.

Another of the more lasting tendencies that indicate the possibility of the emergence of a fragmented world is the swing from liberal to mercantilistic economic policies within and between the industrialized countries. In the present context the most interesting feature here is that in many countries the imposition of restrictions on trade and investment over national boundaries now seems to be accepted as part of the political armoury in a way that would have been unthinkable during the 1950s and the 1960s when the separation of politics and economics was the doctrine of the day. There is frequent evidence now that the opposition to any infringement of liberal economic principles has lost much of its strength, particularly among the great powers. In other words, there has been a break in the trend that had persisted for so long since the end of the war.[12] Many theories have been suggested to explain this change. Some emphasize the character of the people occupying top government positions; others analyze the importance of the expanding public sector—a phenomenon that is common to the whole Western world.

So far we have been concentrating on the role of the national governments in connection with an ethnocentric reaction to the emergence of an international economy. The situation in the trade union world resembles in many ways conditions in the political system. The representatives of the wage-earners also feel threatened by the rise of various bodies commanding a superior range of weapons with which to negotiate; they, too, are used to working in a national environment; they, too, have considerable cultural and political problems and (what is very important) major language problems in their efforts at international collaboration. Furthermore, the disquiet felt in the wage-earner organizations is greater, and is directed towards more immediate problems, than is the case in the political organs. Dissatisfaction with the multinationals is thus likely to come to a head much sooner in the trade union organizations than in the political institutions. We have evidence of this already in the wide gap between trade union opinion and the views of the "administration" in the USA: the latter shows no particular concern when American companies launch out on overseas markets; the former reacts very sharply against "export of jobs," "technological impoverishment" and "unnecessary imports." The American Burke-Hartke Act—a proposal originating in the American trade union movement—is perhaps the best example of a once internationally-minded wage-earner organization switching to a clearly nationalistic path as a result of the MNC problem.[13] In Europe the attraction of the closed solution is counteracted by the internationalism that is built into the ideological roots of the workers' movement, and by the small size of the countries which prohibits extreme isolationist alternatives. But the same sort of tendencies can be identified in Europe on a regional level. The attitude of the EEC towards the rest of the world, for example, is not without its protectionist side.

The European trade union movement is split by political and religious factions, which does make efficient international trade union cooperation more difficult to achieve. However, this difficulty is being gradually overcome as the multinationals gain so much power that the trade union world is being forced to forget its old conflicts. Nonetheless, there are other problems, perhaps of a more fundamental type, which prevent the workers from confronting their employers on an international scale. Practical experience suggests that the opportunities for international cooperation are greatest at the industry level or possibly even at the company level, while the central organs are more sluggish in this respect. This conflict between (a) the traditionally organized trade union pyramid geared towards fair wage negotiations, collective bargaining and cooperation with national political parties, and (b) strong centrifugal forces working for a decentralized bargaining system, has not received as much attention as an obstacle to trade union internationalism as the much discussed differences in political color, religion, and power. In the longer term, however, the fundamental problem of organizational change in the labor movement will be very important. Apart from making a "nationalistic" policy on the part of the central trade union organs more likely, the above dilemma increases the risk of further splits in the national systems.

The closed alternative seems fairly credible when we remember that once a process of this kind gets going, it tends to reinforce itself. The natural reaction on the part of the lagging systems to reduce the increasing complexity of this environment by "closing the boundaries" does not necessarily imply that they are following a nationalistic policy.[14] However, it does seem to be extremely difficult to formulate nondiscriminatory weapons against other countries, particularly because of the short time between perceiving a problem and taking action that is characteristic of the reactive strategy. Thus a process resembling trade warfare can be triggered off by a relatively small number of protectionist decisions.

Economic difficulties in one or more of the major countries would be the most likely trigger. But the small nations, particularly those with an internationally oriented economy, would have the greatest difficulty in surviving in a world of this kind. Nations with large domestic markets would be better prepared to face the harsh conditions.

Thus the restrictive solution may have undesirable side-effects because the consequences go far beyond what was originally intended. But apart from this, there is also reason to doubt the efficacy of this kind of strategy as a way of controlling the MNCs. In the closed world the internationally operating corporations are countered by the actions of individual nations, each one acting for and by itself. In such a world the MNCs might well enjoy considerable advantages over their "opponents:" it would probably be easy for them to find loopholes in the uncoordinated international opposition and even to play the various nations off against one another. It would be very tempting for individual countries to exploit the situation by showing a friendlier face to the MNCs, thereby assuring themselves of special privileges. It is not difficult to envisage a state of abiding competition for the favors of the wicked but rich multinational pirates, which would completely remove the sting from the restrictive policy. The parallel phenomenon of European protectionism in the 1930s comes readily to mind. During that period the European multinationals made great strides in establishing themselves abroad.

This kind of development would not be possible if the national-mindedness and hostility of the countries concerned towards the MNCs were expressions of something more fundamental than a desire to satisfy narrow national interests. For example, it would be difficult for the MNCs to exist at all in a world where the hostility they experienced was based not on nationalistic, selfish arguments but rather on an appreciation of the closed national state as the most suitable environment for human life. If this "nationalism" were to be internationally accepted, no supranational institutions would be allowed to undermine the established order. However, although the "small-is-beautiful" attitude may point in another direction, it seems unlikely that this healthier "nationalism" will triumph over the more materialistic variety. The cultural and political conditions for a Rousseauesque future vary so much from country to country, that anyone deciding to withdraw into the protection of mother nature's bosom is not likely to have many companions there; nor will he receive much encouragement from the more powerful members of the international community.

MNCs AND THE WORLD COMMUNITY—THE REGULATORY SOLUTION

We have already expressed our doubts about whether it is possible to establish a functioning system of control over the multinational corporations, while retaining in other respects present values and policies. An international alternative to the "laissez-faire" world (the *open solution*) would in our opinion be to introduce more *direct* state participation in industrial activities at the international level. There are many ways of doing this, and a number of apparently unrelated factors argue in favor of such a development.

To begin with, the cost of investment in general, and investment in advanced research and development in particular, is rising at such at rate that few individual companies have the necessary resources; nor are they willing to take the accompanying risks. This rise in costs has many causes: some are related to the need to exploit the advantages of scale in a world market that is both physically and politically more accessible than before; others are contingent on the present state of research in the natural sciences where the complexity of the projects demands enormous investments if further progress is to be made. It is significant that most large-scale government engagements in industry recently have concerned projects with heavy capital requirements and long repayment times—nuclear research, defence, space travel, exploitation of the products of the sea, etc.

Secondly, doubts have been expressed particularly during the last ten years about allowing individual private companies to command those resources which, globally speaking, are scarce. This anxiety, rightly or wrongly, has been greatly augmented by the actions of the major oil companies during the "oil crisis." In the last few years there has been a series of specific examples in which various governments, regardless of ideology or political color, have taken action to reduce their countries future dependence on the oil companies. Similar action is already spreading to other raw materials as well.

Apart from anything else it may have done, the oil crisis suddenly, and in a very specific way, made a number of governments aware of their dependence on the assets and politics of other countries, and this insight transformed the problem of scarce raw materials from a game of input-output into hard political realities. There is the fear that private companies may not husband the world's natural wealth satisfactorily; also, competition between the industrial countries for the favors of the nations rich in raw materials is now more open than before, when it was believed that "neutral" companies answered for this distribution. Note, too, that the developing countries usually prefer to discuss with states rather than with companies; in their own countries trade and investment issues are almost always handled at government level.

Thirdly, economic cooperation between East and West is growing rapidly. In many ways this has the same implications for the administration of international business as the preference of the developing countries for centralized negotiations in which decisions are based on a national development plan.

All these factors make it likely that forms of industrial organization will emerge in the near future unlike any that we have known before. In this scenario, nation states and companies appear in a great variety of constellations and, unlike in the controlled laissez-faire scenario, there is no need for formal international agreements. This alternative reflects a very much more "offensive" reaction pattern on the part of the nation states than the two alternatives we have looked at above. The problem of the power of the multinational corporations is solved in passing as it were, in that the state itself steers the internationalization process.

However, since most of the agreements reached and the projects that are initiated necessarily fail to embrace all the countries in the world, there still remains room for what appears in this perspective as the classically simple multinational corporation. If national governments find themselves assuming an increasingly international and active role, then the doubt we previously expressed about the possibility of establishing internationally viable frameworks for the private sector would lose some of its strength, and the remaining multinational corporations of the classical kind would probably be subjected to far-reaching controls.

The forces that are moving us in the direction of this kind of inter-nationalism (i.e., one that is mainly state administered and state regulated) have not very much in common with the forces which are pulling us towards an ethnocentric world. The latter is the result of the shortsighted *reactions*—more or less selfish—to the operations of an apparently threatening and inaccessible international corporate structure; the former represents a proactive and interactive attitude on the part of the political system. We could say that in such a regulatory world the role of the leading system has been transferred from the corporations system to the state authority. At present we designate the multinational corporations as the leading actors because they control technological development; but if the high costs of research and development make it impossible to decentralize R & D in this way, then our theoretical basis logically calls for an investigation of the alternative of state "interference" in the global industrial system.

It is not so easy to establish the role of the trade union system under direct state control of global industrial interdependencies. On the one hand, the above model suggests that the demands of the wage-earner organizations for the consideration of societal interests in the internationalization process will be met. Furthermore, it will be possible to exploit more directly the close connection with social democratic or communist political parties that exists in many countries. On the other hand, the trade union movement will be the only lagging system left on the internationalization merry-go-round. Regardless of the government policy prevailing, this might turn the unions' feeling of powerlessness—which is expressed at present in demands for the regulation of the multinational corporations—against the government system. It, therefore, appears that the regulatory scenario also calls for the inter-nationalization of the trade union system. Apart from extending present collaborative efforts in ICFTU and the international trade secretariats, a likely solution would be to have trade union interests represented directly in specific international projects. Many paths lie open: representation on the boards of the corporations is one way of "forcing" employees to participate in the problems of internationalization. However, this "decentralized" decision structure would certainly not be enough for most trade unionists. Some form of influence on policy-making at the highest level is probably a prerequisite for avoiding the trade union system's support for a protectionist policy. Without some such means of satisfying wage-earner interests, the state authorities would soon come to be regarded as the allies of capital; certain features of the restrictive scenario must therefore be represented even in this basically internationalistic world. To put it briefly, a restrictive *form* may provide the framework for an expansive *content* for overall policy. Some kind of pragmatic approach could satisfy the interests of the central trade union organs in cases where their power is so great that they can only be ignored at the risks of triggering off a wave of protectionism. (However, this model also contains some less attractive elements, which we will discuss in more detail in Chapter 7.)

There is a great dilemma here for the wage-earner organizations that already enjoy considerable power in their own countries. By going ahead with the active administration of the internationalization process, they risk leaving the weaker nations behind. It is not hard to imagine how difficult it would be for the Swedish Confederation of Trade Unions, for instance, to explain to the Spanish Labor Movement why they are supporting the fight for trade union rights in Spain, while at the same time they are sitting on the boards of Swedish multinational corporations, thus approving their activities in Spain and, in the eyes of the illegal Spanish Trade Union Movement, supporting the government in power. The situation would be even more sensitive if the Swedish government were also involved in similar projects. It is hoped, of course, that political control of international industry would provoke changes in the distribution of power and wealth all over the globe. Indeed, it does seem that, if it is not to break down under international tensions, this scenario envisages political power being used in this way and not simply taking over the norms and rules that govern the extraterritorial activities of private business at the present time.

The strength of the regulatory solution as outlined here lies in the fact that it calls, at least on the part of the individual nations, for overall evaluations of the whole internationalization problematique. A weakness is the centralized decision structure which it would almost certainly generate. When the relationships between the interest groups in a society are clearly defined, it is easy to find at the grass-roots level targets for criticism and relatively clear objectives for the various interest organizations. The strategy inherent in the regulatory solution removes much of the justification for the existence of organizations such as local trade unions (in so far as they are not transformed into staff clubs whose interests coincide with those of management, where they are in any case represented). Populist as well as socialist reactions to this kind of society would be very likely to occur, which further confirms the desirability of a certain degree of restrictiveness in the internationalism for large power groups in society.

Much would be gained if the trade union movement could achieve international unity, since the wage-earner organizations could then retain their partisan character and maintain the power of both their central and their local organs. This would leave the poor countries a better chance of making their voice heard than if national central organs—however powerful— were watching over the interests of the wage-earners in consultation with the state and industry. It would also make it less likely that the bilaterally or multilaterally constructed scenario would develop into a kind of "economic-bloc" world in which political tension would increase as every "economic" act becomes interpreted explicitly as "political."

SUMMARY

In this chapter we have tried to analyze the future of the global industrial system according to some possible alternative lines of development. We believe that the internationalization of industry represents a fundamental change in the conditions of existence of the companies themselves and of the groups affected by their decisions. The complexity of the organizational environment, the changes in this environment which call for a transformation of the organizations concerned, the uncertainty about future developments, the need to revise established strategies and make them more flexible, the need to create new institutions and the difficulties this will involve—all these factors make it difficult to study the problems that interest us here from any but very broad and speculative premises. The sum of the separate problems is less than their total implications—what we have called the problematique; the interdependencies are so many and the relationships so complicated that partial or reductionist approaches are of little value.

Our attitude to futures studies (*see* Chapter 3) means that instead of making forecasts of the final outcome of the complicated mechanics and innovativeness of futures-creation, we prefer to try to *conceptualize and specify the choice situation which will confront the decision-maker in the global society*. We have outlined three possible futures (or strategies and strategy outcomes) for lagging systems in the internationalization process. To borrow terms from the Latin-American world, we could say that they represent a striving towards either "dependencia," "independencia" or "interdependencia." The first strategy (if we restrict ourselves to the actions of governments) is exemplified by countries such as Hong Kong, Singapore, the Philippines, Taiwan and to some extent Belgium on the host-country side, and the USA on the home-country side. Apart from some of the socialist countries in Asia, Burma is the best illustration of the independent strategy, with boundaries virtually closed to foreign business interests. The inter-dependent strategy varies from attempts in Australia to "buy back" the country from Great Britain and the USA, to regional solutions such as the efforts of the Andean Pact countries to plan actively for the future of their part of the world and to control and exploit the multinational corporations for their own purposes.

Before developing the methodological consequences of our view in the next chapter, and before describing more specifically the empirical part of our research project, it seems worthwhile to recapitulate some of the crucial elements in our description of the history and possible futures of the emerging global industrial system.

Technological (and economic) development has been the prime driving-force behind the internationalization of business.

Private corporations which through the exploitation, development, production and distribution of goods and services seek to achieve their goals, have been and are at present the leading part in the inter-nationalization process.

Besides the companies there are other systems with economic power, which are influenced by and which participate in this process of internationalization. Two major forces of this kind are the trade union system and the nation state system as manifest in its administrative and political leadership.

While the companies have been able to plan proactively and interactively, other systems have been compelled to inactive or reactive behavior.

Under the pressure of increasingly rapid environmental changes, the three systems will themselves be changed and, above all, the company system will not be allowed to be the sole leading part.

The changes in the system assume various shapes, among which coalitions between and within systems and within and between nations are common. It seems possible to distinguish three strategies for the lagging systems. These are based on accepting *dependence* on the multinational corporations, trying to become *independent* of them or, finally, seeking some form of *interdependence* with them.

Because of the increasing rate of change in the impulses of inter-nationalization, and because of the systems' interactions and their different conceptions of relevant goals, it is fruitless to try to *forecast* how the problematique of the internationalization of business will be "solved."

On the other hand it is essential to try to understand what *alternative* paths developments *may* take, so that by identifying the *present* situation we can help to improve active planning for action in a global industrial system.

NOTES

1. This ties up with the desire of many companies active in several countries to maintain a "low profile." In our interviews the managing directors were often unwilling to attach the label "multinational" to their own companies. "Inter-national," on the other hand, was all right.

2. This type of research provides the basis of several textbooks in international business. An excellent example is S. Robock, and K. Simmonds, *International Business and Multinational Enterprises.* Homewood, Ill.: Irwin, 1973.

3. The UN Report (*see* Chapter 1) contains a discussion of all the current definitions. Perlmutter was the first to use definitions based on attitudes (H. V. Perlmutter, "L'enterprise Internationale: Trois Conceptions," *Revue Economique et Sociale,* Universite de Lausanne. No. 2 Mai 1965). Definitions of this kind now appear to be increasingly prominent, which supports the argument above (*see,* for example, *Business International,* Special Supplement, March 26, 1974, p. 1).

4. *See,* for example, M. Z. Brooke and H. E. Remmers, *The Strategy of Multinational Enterprises; Organization and Finance.* N.Y.: American Elsevier, 1970., and R. Vernon. *Sovereignty at Bay: The Multinational Spread of U.S. Enterprise.* N.Y., London: Basic Books, 1971.

5. For a definition of the concept of leading part, *see* F. E. Emery, "The Next Thirty Years." In F. E. Emery, and E. L. Trist, *Towards a Social Ecology: Contextual Appreciations of the Future in the Present.* London and New York: Plenum Press, 1973.

6. In *Business Eastern Europe,* which comes out every other week, several pages in each number are occupied by lists of newly signed agreements on co-operation between Western and East European interests.

7. The terms inactive, reactive, proactive and interactive have been borrowed from

R. L. Ackoff, "Background of a City's Foreground." Paper presented at Breau sans Nappe, October 1972. In Ackoff's work they designate different attitudes towards planning. We use them here to characterize patterns of actual behaviour.

8. Cf. Emery and Trist, *Towards a Social Ecology*.

9. The concept is developed by Ozbekhan, who defines "problematique" as follows: . . . the idea of an interactive, problematical "situation." In systems language this notion refers to a state that will "deorganize" if nothing is done; namely, if the system is not reorganized at a higher level which represents another system state. (H. Ozbekhan, "Thoughts on the Emerging Methodology of Planning." *unpublished mimeo*, 1973).

10. An investigation of the attitude of the Swedish people to multinational corporations, and their expectations of the future actions of the corporations vis-à-vis Sweden, was carried out at the beginning of 1973 by the Swedish Institute for Public Opinion Research and the business weekly *Veckans Affärer* in co-operation with the authors of this book. The results were published in *Veckans Affärer* no. 16–20, 1973.

11. Cf. A. Sampson, *The Sovereign State of ITT*. N.Y.: Stein and Day Publishers, 1972.

12. This question is discussed further in R. Cooper, "Trade Policy is Foreign Policy," *Economic Impact*, 3/1973.

13. The Burke-Hartke Act contains among other things a suggestion regarding stricter tax regulations for multinational corporations, control of the capital outflow from the USA and possibilities in certain cases of stopping the export of advanced technology from the country. *See*, for example, N. Goldfinger, "The Case for Hartke-Burke," *Columbia Journal of World Business*, VIII (Spring), 1973, pp. 22–26. The suggested law, actually called the Foreign Trade and Investment Act, was presented in 1972 by James Burke and Vance Hartke.

14. Cf. section entitled "Adaptation to Turbulent Environments" in Emery and Trist, *Towards a Social Ecology*.

15. *See* L. Franko, "The Growth, Organizational Structure and Allocative Efficiency of European Multinational Firms: Some Emerging Hypotheses." *mimeo*, Geneve: CEI, 1972.

3

Methodology

In this chapter we will describe the considerations which have governed our choice of method in the study of Sweden's futures in a global industrial system. Further, in more technical terms, we describe how the empirical investigation was carried out. The methods are discussed in considerably greater depth elsewhere.[1]

SYSTEMS VIEW OR PARTIAL ANALYSIS

In Chapter 2 we pointed out that, in studying the future of the global industrial system, it is necessary to take a very broad view and to cast the net geographically wide. The difference between this and a "narrower" view is illustrated in the figures below.

In Figure 3:1, the researcher has an "object of study," for example, the multinational corporation (MNC). Let us now suppose that the trade union movement is interested in evaluating the consequences of MNC operations on variables such as employment, the balance of payments, inflation, etc. — all areas that represent "goal variables" for the wage-earner organizations. Thus, the aim is to seek relations between A (MNCs) and

Figure 3:1

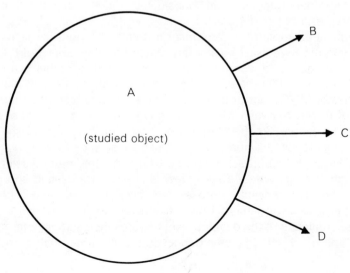

Figure 3:2

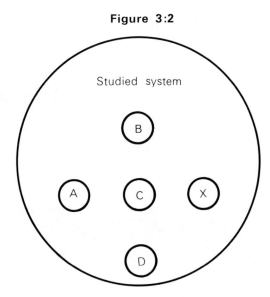

B, C and D. Ideally, B, C and D should be such that they can be easily measured. The effects on nonquantifiable variables are often neglected, at least in practice. The data found are then interpreted in causal terms; "MNCs cause unemployment;" "Inflation makes it easier for MNCs to establish themselves," etc.

Figure 3:2 illustrates an alternative approach. Here the researcher studies a *system*, in which A is only one of many components. This time he has no "object of study" as such, but starts instead from a conception of a whole. He regards the components which together constitute the system as being reciprocally related in a number of possible ways. Causal relationships are regarded as only one of many ways of describing and understanding reality. In so far as the analysis is made in causal terms, complicated relationships such as two-directional causality, aggregation problems and other complex interdependencies are considered more explicitly than in the tradition represented by Figure 3:1.

A typical example of an argument in terms of Figure 3:1 is supplied by a paper from the Swedish Ministry for Industry on the subject of the MNCs.[2] A number of goals for economic policy are listed, together with ways in which MNCs can affect the possibility of fulfilling these goals. It is significant that studies of MNCs, although initiated by a genuine fear of a change in the balance of power between MNCs and governments, for example, are often linked to the Figure 3:1 tradition. This shows the strength of the natural-sciences inheritance still operating in the social science field.

The Figure 3:1 approach might be useful in some natural sciences, and for research in areas where a total view is already established and generally accepted. For our present purposes, however, the Figure 3:2 philosophy must be taken as a fundamental basis for the following reasons.

The complexity of the development towards increasingly interdependent relationships of which the emergence of the multinational corporation is the most significant expression, is so great that a description in terms of causal functional relationships would be meaningless. If it is possible to speak of causal relationships at all, concepts such as multiple and two-directional causality must be introduced. There are techniques for analyzing models allowing for multiple causality at least, but the necessary simplifications and assumptions are very restrictive.[3]

The study of partial relationships, even if these are not interpreted causally, ignores the fact that the nature of an object or an event is determined by its relations with other objects or events. This idea is represented in the Gestalt theory of psychology, which claims that every part of the reality perceived by the individual is interpreted so as to fit into a conception of the whole of which it is a part. Research according to the Figure 3:2 approach tries to allow for this by investigating and interpreting problems in holistic terms. According to this tradition, to understand the nature of the multinational corporations it is necessary to plot the direct and indirect relations between the MNCs and other parts of reality. If we push this view to its extreme, we find that to understand the MNCs we must study *all* objects in reality and all the relations between them. The basis for this would have to be a theory of society at least as a whole. In practice, of course, it is not possible to study everything; instead we have to concentrate on selecting the parts of reality which are crucial to the purpose of the project in question.

The emergence of the multinational corporations is an expression of social changes so deep and so rapid that relationships and explanatory models which were once viable will in future be of doubtful value. An important factor in this context is that identifiable relationships change very quickly; but even more important is the fact that the nature of the "objects of study" themselves and the organizations and people which constitute their environments also change. This means that formulations of research problems which at a given moment seem interesting and well defined, will very soon seem irrelevant.

The attempt to establish partial causal relationships and to construct formal models should be preceded by a detailed definition of the problem. In an area such as ours here—namely, in research into the future interaction between large social systems—there is very little tradition to rely on. Therefore, to ensure against the risk of missing important points in the problematique, we have chosen a broad approach.[4]

Since we view the whole of Swedish society as our "client," we cannot allow ourselves the simplifications which would be possible if we regarded the problems from the point of view of a single organization or group. This applies both to our descriptive base and, even more clearly, to our normative point of departure. Because we believe that the future is moulded in a process whose result is determined by the interactions between various individuals and organizations, and because of our normative purpose, we are compelled to penetrate large and very different areas of reality.

We have kept this plea for a broad systems approach in the study of complex social processes fairly brief. We refer the interested reader to other sources for a more detailed discussion of this view.[5]

METHODS FOR FUTURES STUDIES

As regards method for use in futures studies, we refer to the following classification in Wikstrom and Kordi (1974).[6]

Quantitative methods:
    Tree techniques
    Trend methods:
        Simple regression
        Multiple regression
        Econometric methods
        "Dynamic modelling"

Qualitative or intuitive methods:
    Delphi
    Scenario-writing
    Role play

Tree techniques do not really represent a forecasting method, but a technique of systematization built up according to logical or chronological relations.

All trend methods are based on the principle that future development in the studied area "can be expressed quantitatively, starting from corresponding historical (numerical) values. . . . The common notion, . . . is the belief in some sort of regularity in changes in the socio-technical system."[7] Trend methods are concerned with more or less complex functional relationships of varying degrees of complexity. The forecast variable is assumed to be a function of some other (measurable) variable. It may be a question of causal relationships or simply a function of time. In systems theory terms, we can say that in such models reality is regarded as a *mechanical system.*

In our view, the reality we are studying here must be described as an *innovative system.*[8] Such systems are complex. They alter under the impact of changes in a variety of subsystems. The interdependencies are many-faceted and variable. The researcher does not know all the action variables and possible functional relationships in systems of this kind, as he does (or believes that he does) in systems regarded as mechanical (Cf. Figure 3:1 and Figure 3:2 above). However, the difference between mechanical and innovative systems is not chiefly a question of their complexity. Instead the fundamental difference lies in the fact that reality seen as an innovative system is regarded as open to influence from human (or other purposeful) action. Consequently, concepts such as will, plan, belief, and learning occupy a far more important position than they do when the moulding of the future is seen as a mechanism almost entirely inaccessible to human intervention.[9]

From this extremely summary discussion, it is evident that a trend method would hardly be compatible with the fundamental assumptions which we have stated in Chapter 2 and in the preceding pages. The idea that the studied institutions themselves are changed in the course of a purposeful learning process under the pressure of an increasing mutual dependence is pivotal to our argument.

Since we are not studying mechanical systems, and cannot usefully approximate the systems we are studying to mechanical systems, we are compelled to use what are known as qualitative or intuitive methods. All these methods have in common that the researcher participates in the research process in such a way that he visibly influences the results. Naturally the researcher using quantitative, causal methods also influences the results by his choice of model, of functional relationships, and of data. But the researcher using qualitative methods actually *interacts* with the studied system, with the result that his influence may well be considerable and will certainly be easier to pinpoint.[10]

Starting from a mechanistic conception of reality and of future-creation—and, consequently, relying on trend extrapolation as a forecasting instrument—the possibility of the researcher exerting any influence is normally regarded as a *risk*. However, when the future reality is regarded as the result of a complex interplay between human and organizational wills, it is more in place to speak of the *opportunity* for exerting influence. If the future is seen as something to be created in an innovative system of people, then obviously the researcher too may exercise some influence on developments through his work. There are many examples of self-fulfilling prophesies, and the general view is that they should be avoided as far as possible. Fear of the forecast as a program reflects the desire to explain reality in terms of forces beyond human control and a mechanistic world view. Given our orientation, the relevant question becomes not *whether* but *in what way* and *for whom* the work of the researcher will influence the future. By acknowledging the unavoidably normative aspect of all futurological research, we are forced into a more careful analysis of the function of social science in society.

We have declared that our aim is to improve Sweden's overall futures planning in a global industrial society, by plotting plans for the future and communicating them to different groups in society. Our approach is based on the belief that quicker feedback processes in society with more exact and more relevant information about the reality in the environments of the various organizations really do contribute to "better" action from the point of view of the total system. Thus, we see ourselves—the researchers—not only as collectors of information but also as society's change agents, catalysts of changes in values, synthesizing knowledge rather than analyzing facts.[11] Obviously, even given this belief in the capacity of existing social subsystems to interact effectively, the researchers' own values will still affect their choice of methods and their interpretation of results.

ON INTERPRETING RESULTS IN QUALITATIVE FUTURES STUDIES

One of the most serious and common objections to qualitative futures studies is that the critic has little chance of subjecting the researchers' conclusions to any test based on the material presented. There are many reasons for this. First, a considerable amount of the primary data is *confidential*. Secondly, the interpretation of qualitative data always contains a *subjective element* and alternative conclusions are often possible. Thirdly, every publication of the "results" of a futures study necessarily represents only a rudimentary description of the *research process* that has moulded the researcher's interpretation of what is often a vast array of facts. Fourthly, there is seldom any *theory* underlying futures studies. A theory constitutes a summary of knowledge and provides a starting-point for evaluating the relevance of the data and the correctness of the interpretation.

The "Futures of Sweden" project suffers from all the difficulties that usually hamper futurological research. However, we have tried to improve the reader's chances of evaluating the relevance, the validity, and the reliability of our work in the following ways:

> By presenting primary material in the form of interview summaries and reports on separate phases of the research project, to an extent which is not common in this field. Nevertheless, respect for the confidential nature of much of our material has imposed considerable restrictions on us when it comes to supporting our conclusions by specific reference to our data.

> By reporting changes in our views and methods in the course of the research process (*see* also pp. 57–66 below).

> By stating explicitly the limitations of our technique for processing and synthesizing the data from all the investigated subsystems in the "reference projection" in Chapter 7 (*see* p. 123).

> By reporting in detail our general frame of reference and the somewhat vaguely formulated theories which have guided our work. This is very important. The reader may consider that the "description" in Chapter 2 is reasonably "neutral," but we have explicitly imposed important simplifications by identifying three critical social subsystems (of an endless number of those possible) by regarding the interaction between these systems as the most important factor, by identifying leading parts, and by classifying action opportunities and attitudes in the subsystem on both theoretical and empirical grounds.

Thus, this project is open to criticism from both scientists and laymen to an extent unmatched by most other qualitative futures studies dealing with comparable problems. We will discuss below the question of striking a balance between the presentation of quantitative and qualitative data, and we will show how our sampling procedures may affect the validity and reliability of our results.

METHOD IN "FUTURES OF SWEDEN"

The method we finally chose was an *interview* method using a *scenario* technique; it contained elements of *role play* and had an *iterative* element in its design; in this respect it resembled *Delhpi* studies.[12] The method has been designed by the authors of this book together with Professors' Perlmutter and Trist. The basic idea of using alternative scenarios in interviews with important actors derives from Perlmutter. The fundamental features of the two original scenarios can also be traced back to him. It is partly thanks to Trist that the scope of the study was extended. Trist has also been important to us as a critic and constructive reviewer of our general philosophy, particularly as regards the iterative method and the normative focus.

Bases for Choice of Method

In Chapter 2 we presented the basic assumptions underlying this study. We want to study the way in which three systems—corporations, trade unions and national governments—might be expected to act during the next ten years under the impact of the ongoing internationalization of industry. It is our hope that this will lead to knowledge about the action opportunities available to the systems, and about potential new institutions which may function in the global industrial system of the future. Since parallel studies of the three systems are being conducted in several countries at the same time, we also hope to gain some insight into cultural and institutional dissimilarities between countries, and the importance of these to the future of the global industrial system. Perhaps we can also discover something of the comparative advantages and disadvantages of individual countries in the global industrial system.

In the present study a particularly interesting aspect is Sweden's reputation among many social scientists as a "test laboratory" for new socio-technical ideas, as a country which is relatively homogeneous in several dimensions and is characterized by the strength of the interaction between its social subsystems.[13]

Taking a ten-year perspective as we do here, it seems reasonable to suppose that fundamental changes will appear only if the values which they express have managed to penetrate one or more of the power systems we are studying. Looking even further ahead we can of course assume that new systems will arise to replace the three we have chosen (Cf. Chapter 2). In studies with a more distant time horizon—perhaps 20 to 30 years—it would, therefore, be essential to consider various values prevailing in other groups outside these systems—in political groups, in religious and ethnic minorities, among children, and so on.[14]

The systems' future behavior is determined to a great extent by the knowledge, plans, expectations, attitudes and evaluations of the environment and the home organization entertained by the leading decision-makers in the systems. The future is determined by attitudes to reality and perceptions of reality, rather than by "objective" reality itself.

We have tried here to get some idea of the leading actors' own conceptions of the future: their picture of what the future will look like, what will mould it, and what they believe their own organizations will do.

We can assume that conceptions of the future will differ from person to person within and between systems. We have already suggested that in our view there are several lines of development, any of which may steer future developments. We, therefore, want to confront the actors with *alternative* world views. These world views or scenarios must be designed as *wholes* and not as series of partial assumptions about the future. We believe that the decision-makers react not to individual stimuli but to impressions of wholes. Thus the alternative future views must consist of descriptions of various conditions which are interconnected and which combine to build a totality. We want to register the reactions of the actors to the alternative worlds, thus getting some idea of how they evaluate the probability, the desirability, and the consequences of the alternatives.

By confronting our respondents with alternative world views we not only get some idea of how they would react to the different lines of development; we also *validate* our interpretation of their "own" pictures of the future.

By trying to identify and communicate the leading actors' own envisioned futures, and by registering their reactions to images of the future constructed by ourselves, we can also create and participate in a dialogue between the various systems. Such a dialogue can enrich our description and analysis of the basic views of the actors, and our study of the possible effects of different strategies in the systems. In this way our results provide all the systems with a point of departure for the planning of their future behavior.

We also present a kind of *simulation* of alternatives, making it possible to see the potential effects of different alternatives without actually planning to live through them.

Research design

In light of the above discussion, the empirical section of the study has assumed the following shape:

1. Future views (scenarios) are constructed, describing the three alternative development routes described in Chapter 2.
2. Leading actors in the three systems are interviewed. Their own views of the future and their reaction to the alternative scenarios are charted.
3. Since we have identified the company system as the leading part, the interviews with members of this system are held first. In this way we find out more about the leading system before interviewing members of the "lagging" systems.
4. The other systems studied are the trade union system and, finally, the political system. This order was chosen in accordance with a hypothesis about the degree of "lag" in the three systems.
5. The information obtained in each phase is used as a base for interviews in later phases. In this way the dialogue is enriched and the feedback process between the systems is speeded up.

The design of the investigation is illustrated in the following table.

This step-by-step iterative interview process can continue through several rounds. It would be possible, for instance, to interview smaller groups from the various systems in order to see their reaction to the earlier

Table 3:3

ALGORITHM FOR DESIGN OF THE INVESTIGATION

	System's own world (S)	Open world (O)	Closed world (C)	Regulatory world (Reg)
Business executives (BE)	S(BE)	R_{BE} (O)[1]	R_{BE} (C)	R_{BE} (Reg)[2]
Trade union leaders (TUL)	S(TUL) R_{TUL} S(BE)	R_{TUL} (O) R_{TUL} (R_{BE} (O))	R_{TUL} (C) R_{TUL} (R_{BE} (C))	R_{TUL} (Reg) R_{TUL} (R_{BE} (Reg))
Politicians (P)	S(P) R_P S(BE) R_P S(TUL)	R_P (O) R_P (R_{BE} (O)) R_P (R_{TUL} (O))	R_P (C) R_P (R_{BE} (C)) R_P (R_{TUL} (C))	R_P (Reg) R_P (R_{BE} (Reg)) R_P (R_{TUL} (Reg))

S(BE) refers to the business executives' own world.

R_{BE} (O) refers to the business executives' reactions to the description of the open world.

R_{TUL} (R_{BE} (O)) refers to the trade union leaders' reaction to the business executives' reaction to the description of the open world.

1. The open world used during the interviews with the business executives differed somewhat from scenario O (*see* p. 56).

2. This world view was constructed after the interviews with the business executives had been conducted, for which reason there are no results for the original group of business executives. On the other hand, other groups of business executives were later confronted with the scenario (*see* p. 56).

steps in the process. Interviews with mixed groups or role play exercises would also be possible, to follow up the three steps depicted above. We have limited this report to the three steps indicated in the figure.

On Scenarios

The use of scenarios is of pivotal importance in this investigation. The term "scenario" means different things to different people. For example, it can refer to the result of forecasting activities. "This is how things will be in 1984." It can also mean this, together with a description of how the particular future was achieved. A third alternative is that it covers a description of a particular initial state, and the development of a particular object over time as a function of the initial state. This leaves room for alternative scenarios, since several hypothetical initial states can be included. Military games are of this kind.

In this study we used scenarios as *stimuli in an interview situation*, with a view to *validating* our interpretation of other results, *enriching* the dialogue during the interviews, and *simulating* alternative future courses of action. The simulation idea has much in common with the military variant of the scenario technique, but there is one fundamental difference: the scenarios we use describe a process over time and into the future, while military role games generally *start* from a present state. The use of the scenario technique parallels the holistic systems view which provides the basis for our project as a whole.

The project group designed several scenarios. Five of these were used in the study. They are descriptions of possible future world states according to the three examples of development trends presented in Chapter 2. They describe *possible* future states, without claiming that these are the most probable or that, together, they cover all the possibilities there are.

In view of what we hoped to achieve from our use of scenarios, it was necessary that the design of the scenarios fulfilled certain requirements. The following are the more important of these:

The components constituting the scenario should be regarded by the respondent as mutually consistent.

It must not be possible for the respondent to regard the scenarios as quite improbable.

The scenarios should reflect distinct world states which clearly suggest distinct conditions for the activities of the respondent's organization.

A scenario should appear to reflect the same reality to all respondents.

Scenarios should enrich, not restrict, the respondent's thinking.

Scenarios must be interesting from an "objective" point of view, i.e., they must be perceived as probable and internally consistent by the investigators.

The description of the scenario must be neutral; it should not be burdened by positively or negatively emotive words.

As our starting-point we took four of the scenarios designed by our American sister project group.[15] These were built up around two critical groups of variables. One had to do with whether the policy was *geocentric or ethnocentric*, i.e., basically internationalistic or oriented towards the home country.[16] The other concerned the attitude towards multinational corporations as reflected in political action. This was classified as either *supportive* or *restrictive*. The variables were linked in such a way that geocentricity presupposed a supportive attitude and vice versa. Further, there was a classification according to whether the two Western power blocs (USA, and EEC plus Japan) had similar or dissimilar policies in the relevant respects.

	EEC and Japan, ethnocentric, restrictive	EEC and Japan, geocentric, supportive
USA, ethnocentric, restrictive	I	IV
USA geocentric, supportive	II	III

The four American scenarios were translated and adapted to Swedish conditions. This meant that some items were eliminated and others added. After testing this on a selection of "experts" (researchers and business executives) we came to the following conclusions.

"Unbalanced" scenarios, where the attitude was different between the two blocs, i.e., scenarios II and IV, were considered to have a very low degree of probability because it was not felt that they reflected consistent and reasonably stable world views. Consequently these two worlds were left out of any further discussion.[17]

The two remaining worlds appeared to satisfy the requirements. However, there seemed to be room for a further scenario which had not yet been formulated.

PHASE 1: THE COMPANY SYSTEM

In their final form the interviews with the business executives consisted of three parts:

The respondent's *own view of the future* and his expectations regarding his own company's actions in a ten-year perspective.

Presentation of Scenario 1, the ethnocentric restrictive world. The respondent's reaction to this world (Is it probable? Is it desirable? What works for/against it?) and his expectations regarding his own company's actions, given such a world.

Presentation of Scenario 2, the geocentric world. Reaction to this, etc., as above.

Each time we opened with very general questions, becoming more specific during the course of each interview. Note, too, that the presentations of the scenarios took place *after* the respondent had expressed his own ideas. The reason for this was, of course, to minimize the influence from the interviewer. The interviews took two to three hours. The answers were registered by both the interviewers and, where permitted, on tape. If there was only one interviewer, a tape recorder was always used.

Scenarios
Scenario 1, the ethnocentric restrictive world was presented as follows:

Scenario 1
"In this environment you will meet a generally negative attitude to multinational corporations in Sweden and abroad. Trade policy is protectionistic, and each country's legislation remains independent of foreign conditions. Large companies are viewed with suspicion and the nations try to avoid MNC influence on the national economy. Cooperation between nation states is hampered by an increasingly 'introvert' attitude on the

part of the politicians; activities in organizations such as the UN, OECD, etc., are of diminishing importance."

The situation described in the scenario is assumed to have arisen in the course of a continuous process of development over the next ten years.

Internationally

EEC, Japan and the USA have high external trade barriers.

Unstable exchange rates with frequent crises in the major currencies.

EEC applies antitrust legislation more strictly, and seriously hampers transnational mergers.

No new agreements to eliminate the effects of international double taxation.

Many nations, particularly the developing countries, restrict the scope of private foreign direct investments. Many others insist on local majority ownership and local management of foreign corporations.

Strict control of the export of trained labor on the part of the nation states and EEC.

National legislation regarding the environment makes for very dissimilar conditions in the different countries. The industrial countries are substantially more restrictive than the developing countries.

Trade unions try to prevent the transfer abroad of production units by means of strikes, pressure on government, etc.

Sweden

Sweden protects weak domestic industries and regions by means of high trade barriers. Government buying substantially favours Swedish companies.

Sweden makes private direct investment abroad more difficult for reasons of employment and the balance of payments.

Legislation severely limits the opportunities for foreign companies to buy Swedish businesses.

New legislation makes it very difficult to avoid high taxes by means of intra-company transactions.

Consumers prefer to buy Swedish.

The government puts severe restrictions on the immigration of foreign labor and makes Swedish emigration more difficult.

Legislation regarding the environment applies norms in Sweden that are stricter than those applying abroad.

Trade unions try to prevent companies from moving abroad for reasons of employment."

Scenario 2, the geocentric supportive world was described as follows:

Scenario 2

"This world is characterized by a positive attitude to multinational corporations, both in Sweden and abroad. Further, there is intimate collaboration between nation states and blocs in organs such as the United Nations. The trade blocs' external tariff walls are reduced, a world of free trade is approaching, but even that is not regarded as the final goal. Far-reaching international specialization is considered to be a good thing, and the multinational corporations are seen as suitable tools in these efforts. Consumers buy products without paying any particular attention to their country of origin, the 'international' spirit has also reached the 'people.'

Internationally

EEC, Japan and the USA considerably reduce their external barriers to trade.

Agreement is reached to form a new monetary union with only one currency.

Labor moves freely over borders throughout most of the world.

The developing countries encourage private foreign direct investment, and Japan allows such in 'critical sectors.' New forms for the transfer of capital and technology to the Eastern European countries are created.

Rules concerning the obligations and rights of the multinational corporations are established in the UN.

An environment conference decides upon worldwide norms for the dumping of pollutants, the consumption of energy, etc. Legislation in this sphere is international.

Taxation rules are changed to facilitate international mergers, and 'European company' formation is permitted.

Sweden

Like the other previous EFTA members, Sweden has very close relations with the EEC and harmonizes its social and tax legislation with the EEC.

Sweden introduces a special taxation system for foreign experts resident in Sweden. Free flow of labor to and from Sweden.

The government cooperates with industry to find possible future expansion opportunities for Swedish industry.

Considerable relief as regards private capital export to allow Swedish industry to participate in the international specialization.

Sweden has the same rules as other countries as regards the social obligations of the multinational corporations.

Local trade unions in Swedish-owned multinational corporations cooperate with their foreign equivalents.

Swedish legislation is changed to facilitate international and national mergers."

Sample

The interviews with the business executives were held during the period November 1972—March 1973. In choosing the population for the interviews, we decided that the companies should be active in the manufacturing industry and should have more than two hundred employees.

The final selection in this phase of the project included 48 companies operating in Sweden, of which 8 were foreign-owned. All the companies relevant to our purpose were divided into three groups according to the number of employees in 1971. These groups were:

		Number of companies in the sample	
		Swedish	*Foreign*
(a)	Companies with 200–1,000 employees	16	4
(b)	Companies with 1,000–10,000 employees	14	4
(c)	Companies with more than 10,000 employees	10	—

In groups (a) and (b) 16 Swedish and 4 foreign companies were chosen by means of random selection. In group (c) all 18 companies in the total population were selected. The nonresponse rate was thus 10 companies out of 58, or 17 percent which in view of the respondents we were seeking (managing directors) and the time we intended to occupy (three-hour interviews) can be regarded as satisfactory. In 2 of the 48 companies the respondent was not the managing director—in one case it was the director of long-range planning and in the other the company's only deputy managing director.

The interviews were carried out by a team of four people (among them the two authors of this book) in different combinations. A few interviews were held by one of the authors alone, and in these cases the interview was recorded on tape for further interpretation by some other member of the group.

PHASE 2: THE TRADE UNION SYSTEM

As we shall be reporting in greater detail in Chapter 4, the future expectations of the business executives were very similar to the geocentric supportive Scenario 2, with the major reservation that they expected a more protectionistic development during the next few years. Further, it seemed that no notice was taken of the rudimentary regulation of international business which was included in the description of the scenario.

This motivated a change in the scenarios to be used in later phases of the project. The geocentric supportive scenario was replaced by Scenario A, a summary of the "average" business executive's vision of the future. The ethnocentric restrictive scenario remained as Scenario B. Furthermore we found it necessary to add a Scenario C, describing a geocentric regulatory world, which we found necessary to include in the study. We believe that Scenario C represents a state which many business executives tried to describe. This means that the link established in the American study between internationalism and a supportive attitude to multinational corporations was called in question. A first outline of Scenario C was worked out in our project group as early as August 1972; at that time it was rejected by our American colleagues as totally unrealistic. The version which has been used in the trade union interviews is a revision of this scenario which was tested before being used in the interviews on a group of 35 business leaders, trade union members and politicians.[18]

It is worth remembering that in this round the scenarios did not include any assumptions about the actions of the trade unions, which we expected our respondents would tell us about themselves. Similarly, in the interviews with the business executives nothing was said about how companies behaved in the respective scenarios.

The interviews with the trade union leaders had the same general design as the interviews with the business executives. Now, however, we had three scenarios as against the two we had previously been using. Moreover, in some parts of the interviews we used some of the results from the former interviews to stimulate discussion. Also, the trade union interviews included more questions about the political and economic environment and fewer about the actions of the respondents' own organizations than the interviews with executives.

Scenarios

The following scenario descriptions were used in the trade union interviews.

Scenario A

(Corresponds to the business executives' envisioned world; resembles the previous Scenario 2, the geocentric supportive world):

"The first world, which is expected to prevail in ten years time, is an internationalistic world, in which the nation states cooperate intimately in political and economic affairs and look favorably on an international specialization of production. This world is further characterized by the fact that the corporations have greater freedom to operate internationally than they do at present. There is a positive attitude to international business, and barriers to trade between nations have been abolished, as have restrictions on investment in other countries. This development broke a trend of economic nationalism and suspicion towards the large international companies during the first half of the 1970s. From 1975 onwards there has been a steady development towards a liberal economic policy and a positive view of MNCs as a tool for achieving greater welfare. Sweden has followed the development of the other countries and supports a continued liberal policy, which is thought to favor Sweden's economy. The abolition of barriers to trade and other restrictions is going a little slower between the blocs than within the blocs, but even here developments are moving steadily towards greater integration.

Below we give some *examples* of what could characterize a world of this type:

Internationally

EEC, the USA and Japan have reduced their external tariffs.

Labor moves freely across borders in practically all parts of the world.

The developing countries encourage private foreign direct investment, and Japan allows foreign investment also in 'critical sectors.'

Increasing economic co-operation between the Eastern European countries and the West.

An increasing number of companies whose ownership and operations are spread over the greater part of the world.

Sweden

Sweden has very close relations with EEC; harmonizes its social and taxation legislation.

Government and industry cooperate in finding possible future expansion opportunities for Swedish industry.

It is easier now for Swedish companies to invest abroad and for foreign companies to invest in Sweden.

Swedish companies cooperate much more with companies abroad.

The purchase of companies across national borders is on the increase. Swedish companies are becoming increasingly dependent on foreign markets for both sales and production."

Scenario B

(Corresponds to the earlier Scenario 1, the ethnocentric restrictive world)

"This world is characterized by an increasingly introverted attitude on the part of the politicians and the nations. Cooperation in bodies such as the UN, OECD, etc., is becoming less important, and economic policy is becoming increasingly protectionistic as a result of a successive escalation of economic restrictions between trade blocs and nations. There is a generally negative attitude towards the multinational corporations in most countries; people dislike foreign influence over their national economies. It is assumed that this situation has evolved in an unbroken trend throughout the 1970s.

Below we list *examples* of conditions which could characterize this type of world:

Internationally

EEC, the USA and Japan have high tariffs and other barriers to trade.

Unstable rates of exchange with frequent crises of important currencies.

It becomes more difficult for corporations to buy companies in other countries.

Many nations, particularly developing countries, restrict the volume and scope of private foreign direct investment. Many others insist on local majority ownership and local management of foreign corporations.

Strict control on the part of governments of the inflow and outflow of labor.

National environmental legislation leads to very varying conditions in different countries. The industrial countries are very much more restrictive than the developing countries.

Sweden

Sweden protects weak domestic industries and regions by high barriers to trade. Government purchasing clearly favors Swedish companies.

Sweden severely restricts private direct investment abroad on grounds of employment and balance of payments.

Legislation makes it very difficult for foreign enterprises to buy up Swedish companies.

Government limits immigration of foreign labor and emigration of Swedish workers and experts.

Environmental legislation imposes norms in Sweden that are stricter than those applying abroad."

Scenario C

(The geocentric, regulatory world)

"In this world the national governments have recognized a conflict between an efficient world economy and the sovereign nation states. This has led to an increasing number of internationally agreed upon rules for the control of the multinational corporations. The world as a whole is internationally oriented, and there has been a marked relaxation of political tension. The nations seek global solutions to problems such as environmental conservation, energy supply and global income distribution. There is a rapid increase in direct cooperation between the nations on industrial matters, while cases of obvious abuse of economic power on the part of some large multinational corporations have led to stricter controls of private business over national borders.

Below we list *examples* of conditions which could characterize this world

Internationally

Some of the very large MNCs are divided into several smaller units.

Most developing countries agree not to accept direct foreign investment, unless national majority ownership is guaranteed.

All MNCs with more than 50,000 employees must report to an international commission which investigates every corporation's total contribution to the economic and social development of the world.

Company plans are also reviewed.

All barriers to trade in the Western world are abolished. Trade with the Eastern countries is increasing rapidly.

All aid to developing countries passes through the United Nations.

The industrial countries donate half their annual GNP growth as development aid.

Sweden

The National Swedish Pension Insurance Fund is used for acquiring ownership in most of the Swedish MNCs. In certain cases there is also some foreign state ownership.

Foreign companies are not allowed to buy *dominating* ownership in Swedish-owned companies.

The companies' investments are governed by long-range state planning.

Sweden participates in an international project for solar energy led by the UN. Both private and state-owned companies from many different countries are involved in the project.

As in other countries, employees and the state are represented on the boards of companies."

Sample

The trade union interviews began at the end of September 1973. The last interview was held at the beginning of December. Our sample included the central management of both the Swedish Confederation of Trade Unions (LO) and of the Swedish Central Organization of Salaried Employees (TCO) and, in the case of LO, also the leaders of the unions most affected by internationalization and a selection of shop stewards from large internationally operating companies, both Swedish-owned and foreign-owned. In the latter group the nonresponse rate was about 30 percent, mainly because it was difficult to find times that suited both respondent and interviewer. Non-responses in the TCO and the LO groups amounted in both cases to one person and can, therefore, be regarded as insignificant.

Number of people interviewed:

TCO	6
LO, central	6
LO, unions	11
LO, local branches	10
	——
	33

The interviews were conducted by one or two interviewers and at least one of the authors was always present. This time no tape recorders were ever used, since several of the respondents at the pilot interviews had rejected the idea. The interviews generally lasted about three hours.

PHASE 3: THE POLITICAL SYSTEM

In this round of interviews we were dealing with the people whose task it is to transform the interests of the citizens—the voters—into political action. Strictly speaking this should have meant making our selection from among members of the Riksdag (the Swedish parliament).[19] However, we felt that because we were trying to establish the future as envisaged by those holding the ultimate power in the various systems, we ought also to include members of the government and—although they are not formally politicians—highly placed civil servants in government departments.

Scenarios

We used the same scenarios as we had used in the trade union interviews. Our analysis of the data from these interviews gave no grounds for a further revision of the scenarios. The design of the interviews was also the same, except that certain institutional dissimilarities had to be allowed for.

Sample

In selecting interview subjects from among members of the Riksdag we tried to achieve a representative political sample, but we also looked for people who would presumably be well informed about the problems that interested us. In operational terms this meant that we chose the chairman or the vice chairman of committees relevant to the internationalization of industry. To these we added all the party leaders and a few more committee members, so that all political shades would be represented. Four people dropped out either because they could not spare the time or because they did not know enough about the subject. This left 16 interviewees from the Riksdag. There were 3 from the moderate party (= the conservative party), 3 from the liberal party, 2 from the centre party (= the agrarian party), 7 social democrats and 1 from the communist party.

From the government we chose 7 cabinet ministers who seemed likely to be most closely affected by internationalization, and 7 under-secretaries (or the equivalent), all of whom were members of a working group appointed in March 1973 to consider various aspects of the multinational corporation problem. Nonresponses here were 2 cabinet ministers and 1 under-secretary. Thus, as in earlier phases of the project, nonresponses were gratifyingly and surprisingly low. We were fully aware that we were expecting very busy people to subject themselves to long and difficult interviews. And it should be noted that the leaders of all the five political parties represented in the Riksdag were among those we were able to interview.

Number interviewed:

Riksdag	16
Government	5
Under-secretaries	6
	——
	27

The interviews were held between January and March 1974, and two interviewers—including at least one of the authors—were always present. Each interview lasted for 2–3 hours. They were not recorded on tape, but the two interviewers wrote independent reports directly after the interviews.

ON THE PRESENTATION AND INTERPRETATION OF DATA

These long and generally rather loosely structured interviews provided mainly qualitative data, which had to be interpreted by the researcher/interviewer. A good deal of the interpretation consisted of registering arguments and identifying the values expressed. Some of the material was interpreted on attitude scales (for example, the respondents' view of policies on international business). Finally, some answers were more in the nature of "hard data," mainly general expectations about such things as the corporations' (or the respondent's own company's) foreign commitments and the growth of the economy. Here the interpretation problem consisted of making the point of the question clear to the respondent and of controlling that he/she had really answered the question asked. This sometimes called for supplementary information or a more specific definition of questions; and meant reminding the respondent occasionally of the difference between *expectations* (sometimes conditioned) and *hopes*.

Obviously, response patterns varied, even between individual people in the groups reported separately in Chapters 4–6. It was also probable that individual responses ranged over a scale from well-founded expectations to pure guesses.

The business leaders interviewed included the managing directors of 10 of the 17 largest Swedish industrial enterprises (measured in number of employees), and a stratified sample of smaller companies, both Swedish-owned and foreign-owned. If we look at the way the final selection is actually distributed, we find that 20 of the 40 largest industrial companies are represented, or, in other words, a major part of Swedish industry as a whole. Together the companies interviewed had about 400,000 employees in 1972. Thus the selection is representative, in that companies employing almost half the workforce of Swedish industry are included. On the other hand, we have excluded altogether companies with fewer than 200 employees, which means that no conclusions regarding this numerically large group can be drawn from the present study.

In the trade union system our selection was as good as complete (i.e., including the whole population) at the central and the union level. At the shop steward level, the sample was geared to large companies with extensive international operations.

The political sample was complete as regards party leaders and members of the special working party referred to (with the exception of one person), and almost complete with regard to government departments directly affected by the internationalization of business. Among members of the Riksdag our selection was on the whole smaller, but did include the "trendsetters" in each party, i.e., those who occupy the key positions on committees.

It is thus highly probable that even the small differences that appear between relatively homogeneous groups in the sample do actually represent dissimilarities in views between the groups and are not just a random phenomenon. (It could also be claimed that what a party leader or a trade union leader says *is* identical with the standpoint of the party or the union and, as we have seen, our sample is larger than just these leaders.)

In the following presentation and analysis of results we include no measures of standard deviations or levels of significance, this for a variety of reasons: first, to avoid overloading our text; secondly, because the intricate problem of identifying the three populations would itself require a comprehensive analysis, and we do not consider this important enough to warrant inclusion; thirdly—and this is the most important reason—the aim and purpose of this kind of future study (i.e., to examine present values, expectations and plans in order to try to identify consonances and dissonances with implications for the future) implies an interest in what Emery & Trist[14] have called "emergent processes." One way of identifying processes of this kind is to study just such small and possibly very recent dissimilarities in the attitudes of different groups. These differences are often not such as to lend themselves to quantification; they can be expressed only in qualitative form, which means that they cannot be exposed to statistical testing for significance. Thus there is a risk that the search for emergent processes may result in over-interpreting differences which are no more than pure random variations. However, the futures researcher must take this risk. Others can subsequently judge whether it was justified. In the present case we have found clear support in the qualitative part of our interviews for the differences in quantified expectations reported in the analysis, and vice versa. The qualitative analysis is the most important. However, we believe that the many frequency tables and mean-value tables with which we illustrate our results will provide the reader with a convenient summary of some of our main points.

NOTES

1. *See* G. Hedlund, *Det Multinationells Företaget, Nationalstaten och Fackförenin-Garna—en Diskussion av Utgångspunkter och Metoder.* (*The Multinational Corporation, the Nation State, and the Trade Unions—A Discussion of Points of Departure and Methods*). Stockholm: EFI Publishers, 1976.
2. *Multinationella Företag.* Stockholm: Industridepartementet, 1973, *mimeograph*.
3. *See* for example H. M., Blalock, *Causal Inferences in Nonexperimental Research.* Chapel Hill, N.C.: University of North Carolina Press, 1964.
4. An interesting discussion on the possibility of building formal models for simulating social conflicts is to be found in M. Norton, C. K. Mitchell, and F. R. Javes, "The Systems Analysis of Conflict," *Futures*, April 1974.
5. *See*, for example, C. W. Churchman, *The Systems Approach.* N.Y.: Delta Books, 1968, for a straightforward introduction to systems theory. *See* also Hedlund (1976) for an application to this particular study.
6. S. Wikström, and I. Kordi, "Omvärldsprognoser och Tekniker Härför." (Environ-

mental Forecasting and Applicable Techniques). Stockholm: University of Stockholm, *mimeo*, 1974.

7. Wikström and Kordis, pp. 13–14 (own translation).

8. For a discussion of the distinction between mechanical and innovative systems, *see*, for example, J. Annerstedt, and L. Dencik, "Koloniseringen av Framtiden." (The Colonialization of the Future). *Ord och Bild*, 6/1971.

9. After this report was written we were exposed to the distinctions between different types of systems developed by R. L. Ackoff, and F. E. Emery, in *On Purposeful Systems*, London: Tavistock, 1972. We believe this work admirably clarifies what we try to say in our discussion of mechanical and innovative systems. In their terms, we look at our "objects of study" as purposeful systems.

10. In the natural sciences it has long been known that the observer affects his study object, sometimes in ways that do not allow for "adjustment." The "uncertainly principle" of Heisenberg expresses this "problem" very well.

11. In psychology and business administration research, the concepts of "change agent" and "action research" have become accepted labels for researchers and research with a normative orientation. What we have tried to do in "Futures of Sweden in the Global Industrial System" is to function as change agents at the societal level. This means that the researcher role, which at the level of client research is already very complex, becomes even more multifaceted.
    There is a very interesting discussion of the role of social science research in the future, with an argument for both the systems viewpoint and the normative orientation, in F. E. Emery, and F. L. Trist, *Towards a Social Ecology—Contextual Appreciations of the Future in the Present*. London and N.Y.: Plenum Press, 1973. Chapters 1 and 7 are particularly relevant in this context.

12. In *role plays* the object of study is expected to act as he would if certain given conditions prevailed. *Scenarios* are generally descriptions of imagined future states. *Iterative* means in steps. *Delphi studies* use panels of experts, in which the experts are asked to make forecasts—for example they may be asked when a particular invention will appear. The results of the first round of individual forecasts are put together and sent back to the experts, who are then asked to revise their earlier forecasts. This iterative process can be repeated several times, and the aim is generally to get the forecasts to converge.

13. *See*, for example, Emery and Trist, *Towards a Social Ecology*, pp. 207–208 and L. N. Lindberg, "A Prospectus for Political Futures: The Theory and Practice of Post-Industrial Society." University of Wisconsin, mimeograph, 1973.

14. Cf. the "Development Space," in E. Jantsch, *Technological Forecasting in Perspective*, Paris, OECI), 1966 and "The Early Detection of Emergent Processes" in Emery and Trist, *Towards a Social Ecology*, pp. 24–37. The original design of this study included depth interviews with homogeneous and mixed groups of people who can be expected to represent new values not embraced by the three powerful systems. Due to lack of resources this part of the project had to be replaced by the previously mentioned enquiry conducted by the Swedish Institute of Public Opinion Research concerning the Swedish people's expectations of, and attitudes to, the internationalization of industry.

15. *See* H. V. Perlmutter, F. R. Root, and L. Plante, "Responses of U.S.-Based MNCs to Alternative Public Policy Futures," *Columbia Journal of World Business*, 8, (Fall), 1973, pp. 78–86.

16. The terms ethnocentric, polycentric and geocentric were first coined by Perlmutter as descriptions of attitudes in leadership style in the MNCs. (H. V. Perlmutter,

"L'enterprise Internationale, Trois Conceptions," *Revue Economique et Sociale*, 2, 1965.)

17. The American project group, too, came to the same conclusion after pilot interviews.

18. *See Futures of Sweden in a Global Industrial System*, report from an IFL-seminar, April 1973. Mimeograph.

19. Sweden's Riksdag is directly elected by the voters every three years. In 1973 everybody over 20 years of age had the right to vote. (The age has now been lowered to 18). More than 80 percent of the electorate voted. Elections are strictly proportional, apart from a rule to the effect that a party which does not gain at least 4 percent of the popular vote (or 12 percent in a geographical district) will not be represented in the Riksdag. In 1973 the 350 seats were distributed as follows:

Social Democrats	156
Center Party (formerly the Agrarian Party)	90
Moderate Party (Conservatives)	51
Liberal Party	34
Communist Party	19
	350

The Social Democrats have been in power—sometimes with a coalition partner and rarely with a majority of their own—since 1932. By tradition civil servants are not appointed to government departments and government agencies on political grounds. They are regarded as experts, and are expected to be loyal to the sitting government.

4

Business Executives' Visions
of the Future

Business executives in Sweden expect the internationalization of Swedish industry to continue. This theme runs through all the interviews with the 48 top executives. They "believe in Sweden," admittedly, but the majority of them regard the domestic market as too limited. The slogan "growth at home through growth abroad" well reflects the views of the business community.

Furthermore, the Swedish business leader also looks forward to developments over the next ten years with some confidence. His vision includes neither great dreams nor fears for the future. He sees as reasonable and probable those developments that will benefit his own company. Nonetheless, expectations about the business climate of the future vary considerably from one businessman to another. What they all seem to have in common is a belief that their own particular company will manage to survive satisfactorily.

COMMENTS ON PUBLIC POLICY TOWARD
INTERNATIONAL BUSINESS

It appeared from our interviews that the companies' expansion plans, with very few exception were directed towards foreign markets. Disturbances on this front were generally regarded as a very serious matter. Table 4.1

Table 4:1

CONSEQUENCES OF THE LOSS OF FOREIGN MARKETS
40 SWEDISH COMPANIES

What do you think the consequences would be for your company of a withdrawal from all international activities?

Catastrophe (the company's survival threatened)	19
Permanent damage	16
Would require extensive adjustments (serious, but not permanent)	4
Would call for some little adjustments (awkward, but not serious)	1
No negative effects	0

gives some idea of the gravity with which the business executives viewed the consequences of a loss of foreign markets.

To be completely cut off from foreign markets would result in very big structural changes in Swedish industry. "We would simply not be the same company," was a common comment from our respondents, most of whom soon began to talk of the disadvantage to Sweden of a restrictive economic climate. As a small, highly industrialized country with substantial exports and imports, Sweden is dependent on a world in which production factors and goods move relatively freely over national borders.

According to our respondents, internationalization of industry is by no means a Swedish phenomenon. In fact many of them pointed out that it may go more quickly in other countries. Some of them suggested that, up to now, Sweden may have been a few steps ahead of many other nations with regard to its attitude to the internationalization of business. The traditionally liberal trade policy was only one sign of this. Some others, however, were a little ironic about the picture of Sweden as a pioneer in all sorts of fields.

In particular, the Sweden of social welfare and taxation policy "has been rather complacent," "has run ahead," "is a marginal country which must pay more attention to the frames of reference of other countries." However, even this group regarded Sweden as an "honest country" in an international context, and were very ready to contrast Sweden's stable attitude to, for example, "France's short-sighted and egoistic actions." On the whole, though, there was a tendency in the answers to regard Sweden as somewhat more restrictive than other countries, particularly as regards direct investment over national borders. (Cf. Table 4:2.)

There was a marked difference, particularly among the leaders of the

Table 4:2

"HOW WOULD YOU DESCRIBE SWEDEN'S PRESENT POLICY AND THAT OF OTHER COUNTRIES, AND HOW DO YOU THINK IT WILL BE IN 10 YEARS TIME IN THE FOLLOWING AREAS? CONSIDER ALL THE TIME HOW THIS POLICY WILL AFFECT YOUR COMPANY."

Scale 1–5 (1 = very liberal; 5 = very restrictive)
(n = 40)

	Sweden		Abroad	
	1972	1982	1972	1982
Trade policy	2.3	2.1	3.3	2.5
Policy in the home country towards the investments of companies in other countries	3.0	2.9	2.6	2.6
Policy in the host country towards the investments of foreign companies	2.6	2.5	2.0	2.0
Policy towards the immigration and emigration of labour	2.8	2.9	2.8	2.5

larger companies, between the description of policy in general and policy as it affected their own companies. A typical expression of this difference is the following statement, varieties of which were often heard: "Getting permission for foreign investment is almost impossible, but *we* have never had any problems."

The majority of our respondents believed that, looking ahead ten years, the trend in Sweden and other countries will be towards greater liberalization. By and large they envisaged a world with fewer restrictions on the flow of goods, labor and capital. They also expected to see a considerable increase in cooperation between countries, trade blocs and companies, but *not* between the trade unions of different countries. Many also expected the rate of company growth to be somewhat higher than it is today. (We should note here, however, that the method we used may have had something to do with this. We have the same phenomenon when a population forecast based on aggregates of county plans predicts a rapid increase of several millions in the population of Sweden).

The main reason given for this trend was the enormous economic advantages that an increase in international specialization would bring. Internationalization would also lead to such strong mutual economic dependence that there would be less risk of an increase in political tension. Looking forward a little further, one circumstance which was felt to be important was the positive attitude towards international issues which was said to prevail among the younger generation. Sweden's young "have a basically liberal view," "want to have free-and-easy international relations," "would be hard hit if restrictions increased."

Nevertheless, it is important to note that few of our respondents dared to hope that this development would be uninterrupted. A great many business leaders envisaged a marked swing away from the long-run trend towards greater internationalization around the middle of the 1970s: nationalistic trends caused by employment problems and raw-material crises that may lead to a period of harsher inter-country economic restrictions.

Most executives regard such fluctuations as normal—"the curve wobbles a bit"—and are therefore convinced that the tendency will lose impetus as the various groups concerned recognize that a more open policy is to be preferred. Any really persistent nationalism is regarded as "an unthinkably retrograde step," or as one business executive commented: "In the end internationalization must come; Swedes are *really* nationalistic nowadays only when they watch ice hockey."

Nonetheless, even a temporary ethnocentric policy would have considerable negative consequences, particularly for small countries like Sweden. "In a country as small as ours, neither companies nor public authorities can afford to isolate themselves"; "Our knowledge would suffer"—these were typical comments. Consequently the executives, with one or two exceptions, did not think that "anyone"—i.e., government authorities or trade unions in Sweden—would support a policy of this kind. Instead they often mentioned that the greatest threat to continued internationalization comes from the big countries and the major blocs, which have a better chance of surviving in a more restrictive world. Several mentioned the USA, but also the EEC countries (France and Great Britain in particular) as possible seats of nationalistic disturbance. The desperate situation in certain of the developing countries was also cited by several respondents as a possible source of increasing nationalism in the world.

THE BUSINESS EXECUTIVES—FUTURE PLANS

Markets and Location

In individual companies the future is expected to bring considerable expansion abroad. These executives' plans include a substantial increase in the importance of sales to other countries and in the amount of production and development work located abroad. (*see* Tables 4:3 and 4:4.) This does not mean that the absolute size of operations in Sweden will fall. The business executives, without exception, see the foreign operations as a necessary adjunct to operations in Sweden.

Table 4:3

PERCENTAGE OF SALES, PRODUCTION AND R & D ABROAD—40 SWEDISH COMPANIES

	Situation today (1972)	The business executives' forecast 1982
Proportion of sales abroad (per cent of total sales)	55%	69%
Proportion of production abroad (per cent of total production)	17%	31%
Proportion of research and development work abroad (per cent of total R & D)	10%	28%

(All the figures are unweighted mean values of the answers of the 40 Swedish executives included in the study.)

Table 4:4

PERCENTAGE OF PROFITS DERIVED FROM FOREIGN OPERATIONS (EXPORT AND OVERSEAS PRODUCTION)— 40 SWEDISH COMPANIES

Proportion	Year	
	1971	1982
0 — 10%	4	1
11 — 25%	7	2
26 — 40%	5	7
41 — 60%	10	7
61 — 100%	14	23

If we look at the individual companies, we find that only 6 of them (or 15 percent of the sample) are expecting a lower volume of production in Sweden in ten years time, while the others are expecting an increase in production on the domestic market as well as abroad. Almost all the business executives see a positive relationship between foreign and Swedish operations, and in this their view contrasts sharply with the belief in at least limited substitutability expressed by trade union representatives and politicians (*see* Chapters 5 and 6).

International expansion is predominantly directed towards Western Europe. North and South America also appear in the answers, as do the Eastern countries, but in the latter cases generally only with very marginal amounts. It is very striking that the oil states and the developing countries in general, for example, were hardly mentioned at all at the interviews.

Internationalization was said to be dictated chiefly by the need to get closer to the customer. Other reasons for internationalizing production, such as lower labor costs, transport problems and trade barriers, were sometimes mentioned but were not thought to be as important. It was felt that location would be increasingly governed by markets in future; that it was becoming more and more difficult to maintain competitive strength without production companies on the most important foreign markets at least. To this was added the need to protect against risk. By locating production on local markets a company protects itself from a possible rise in tariffs, which might, in such circumstances, even favour the company.

There are also plans to locate considerably more research and development (R & D) abroad. This shift also reflects a desire to get closer to important markets. However, it seems that costs in Sweden are more important in choosing a location for R & D than in choosing a location for production. The high marginal taxes in Sweden were often mentioned as a reason for taking research work to foreign experts instead of trying to persuade experts to move to Sweden from abroad. Furthermore, rapidly rising costs and specialization have highlighted the importance of purchasing knowledge particularly from abroad, and of various forms of international cooperation in the R & D field.

Organization and Ownership

All sorts of new forms of collaboration clearly represent an important part of company strategy for the future. Thus, as many as 96 percent (i.e., all but two) of our respondents imagine that their companies will be engaged in more collaborative agreements in ten years time than they are today.

They foresee agreements of many different kinds—from jointly owned companies to temporary commitments in specific development projects. For fear of losing their identity some of the smaller companies appeared to be slightly doubtful about this trend. At the same time everything suggests that they have accepted more cooperation as an inevitable part of their future, and they prefer it to the idea of being taken over. For the larger companies, on the other hand, collaborative agreements already appear to be an established part of their strategy, a way of saving resources in a world where specialization is becoming increasingly necessary.

Our results show that company organization will be changed in other ways too, mainly in connection with the internationalization process. For example, it is expected that:

there will be an increase in foreign ownership of Swedish parent companies

there will be more local ownership of subsidiaries abroad

there will be more foreigners in key positions in the companies

there will be more cooperation with various authorities and trade unions at home and abroad.

Various factors are suggested to explain the increase in foreign ownership. According to the large companies, ownership is going to become more dispersed as a result of quotation on foreign stock exchanges. The medium-sized companies expect that various kinds of joint ventures with foreign companies will eventually lead to an increase in foreign ownership. The relatively small family-owned companies where there is no natural successor to the chief executive are in a rather special situation. Among those which consider selling out when the time comes for a change of leadership, because of inheritance tax, many seem to expect that the buyer will be a foreign company.

As regards foreign subsidiaries, most respondents say they would *prefer* to own them 100 percent. However, they expect an increase in local ownership to become inevitable as a result of financial and political restrictions. As regards the possibility of controlling subsidiary operations, any wish to integrate the operations of the whole corporation are thwarted by the same obstacles. Admittedly an overwhelming majority say they would like to aim at more decentralization, but by this they seem to imply little more than extensive delegation of the right of decision on operational matters.

Thus nothing suggests that the business executives regard these changes in organization and ownership as altogether desirable. In fact they seem to regard them as a necessary adjustment to the future world they expect to see. However, to judge from the results of our American sister project, it appears that in an international context Swedish business leaders have an unusually open attitude to new forms of organization and new collaborators, and to changes in power relationships.

Relations with Government Authorities and Trade Unions

The most notable feature of our discussion with the business executives about the government authorities and the trade unions was their eagerness to reply very diplomatically to direct questions about possible cooperation over the next ten years. "We must go hand in hand;" "We are all in the same boat;" "Always keen to have good relations;" "Good relations are essential" — these were typical answers and there were a great many more in the same strain.

This reaction, perhaps, mainly reflects an established Swedish tradition. But it probably has other explanations too. The conditions for such an attitude are more favorable in a small, highly developed and homogeneous country liké Sweden than they are in many other countries. Thus, by and large, it seems that our executives really do believe in good relations, both with government authorities and trade unions, and contacts with these bodies are likely to increase a good deal.

There was a marked difference between the small companies and the large corporations when it came to their attitude to politicians and public authorities. While the former seemed to think that the government and other political organs were controlled by a malevolent and hostile "them," the latter were far more understanding. Admittedly the executives in the largest companies said that politicians had to take a short-run rather than a long-run view and had to adapt their behavior to the demands of their not always well-informed voters; but these executives also understood this and said that in almost all cases it was possible to discuss matters with the politicians. The leaders of smaller companies found it very much more difficult to see the actions of the politicians as anything other than "crazy impositions," and as "an expression of their lack of understanding for our problems."

Since the politicians are "protecting their seats" and "don't want to lose the power they have," development towards an international world is to some extent slowed down but, say the business executives, politicians will eventually come to realize that internationalism is the only way to satisfy national interests. This view of the political decision-makers as men motivated by rather crass attitudes was very common among the business executives. Both the geocentric and the ethnocentric worlds (see Chapter 3) were seen as the result of the exploitation of limited national and personal interests, rather than of ideologically important decisions. Perhaps the executives' vision of the future can best be described on this point as a "self-interested geocentric" world. Thus the majority expected more voluntary interaction between companies and the Swedish authorities; they were also positive in their view of future contacts with foreign authorities. Hardly anyone quoted any negative experience of their foreign government contacts.

If we are to believe the majority, relations with the trade unions are going to be good all along the line. Nobody envisaged any policy of confrontation. One group was particularly benevolent in their view of the local trade unions, and thought the "bigwigs" and "theorists" at the central level were much more dangerous. This attitude was common among the small businesses, particularly the small country-based manufacturing companies. Another group, mainly representing the large companies, emphasized the knowledge and responsibility shown by the central organs, and contrasted this with wild-cat strikes and similar irresponsible action on the extreme left. "The leadership of LO is educated and intelligent;" The worst thing that could happen would be for the leaders to lose control." The top men in the large Swedish companies were generally positive in their attitude to the whole Swedish trade union movement. They all regarded the Swedish trade unions as more enlightened, more cooperative and more internationally minded than foreign trade unions: "They understand the companies;" "They are a stabilizing factor;" "The best trade unions in Europe."

In general the business executives did not envisage any really extensive cooperation among unions on the international plane. They referred to ethnic, political and religious differences between the unions in the different countries. Many of them declared that national trade unions are really only interested in increasing their members' wages, and that international solidarity would consequently "only be a function of self-interest"—as it is for the politicians and the voters.

Nor, except in a few cases, did the executives see an internationalization of the trade union movement as anything particularly desirable. Their positive attitude towards trade unions seems in most cases to refer to contacts on the home front. Many of them were clearly afraid of what would happen if the Swedish trade unions were to "cooperate too much with the immature trade unions of other countries." "The Swedish trade unions might get like the Americans;" "They would get too bureaucratic and political;" "You never know what the foreign bigwigs have in mind." Among the companies which were on the brink of increasing their investments abroad, the negative attitude towards the internationalization of the trade unions was particularly marked. There was also a fear that the local trade unions might react negatively to changes in the company. These particular executives also tended to believe in an increasingly negative attitude on the part of the trade unions towards their companies' activities abroad; "The trade union thinks that everything should be as it has always been. They want to feel safe and calm. They realize there must be some development, but they don't want it to affect them. At bottom they have an extremely inert and conservative attitude."

"Cooperation between management and unions—the best is what we've already had," said one of our respondents. And many business executives would perhaps agree if they believed, as he did, that the internationalization of the trade union movement was almost upon us. However, for most of them a strongly international trade union movement was a distant prospect, and at present they had no anxiety about a deterioration in relationships.

BUSINESS EXECUTIVES ON THE SCENARIOS— PROBABILITY AND DESIRABILITY

When the first phase of the interview study was complete, i.e., when the respondents had given their "unprovoked" views of the world and the future of their own companies, two worlds or scenarios constructed by the research group were presented. The first of these can be described as restrictive and ethnocentric from the point of view of the companies, the other as supportive and geocentric. (The scenarios are described in Chapter 3.)

A comparison of the executives' perception of the future with these two scenarios shows that "their" world has many features in common with the geocentric, company-prone world. The main difference is that the rudiments of control over the multinational corporations at a global level as outlined in the geocentric scenario had no equivalent in the respondents' own thinking and tended to be "forgotten" in discussing the scenario. Thus, the geocentric world was judged to be the most probable by most of the business executives. The average probability that this world would be realized by 1982 was about 40 percent, while the corresponding probability for the ethnocentric world view was a little over 25 percent. Eight respondents considered it totally unlikely that the latter world would prevail by 1982, while two of them did not believe in the geocentric world at all.

We have mentioned before that a great many of the business executives envisaged a process which was characterized by increasing ethnocentrism and restrictiveness to start with, but which would move in the direction of a more open world of the geocentric type towards the end of the 1970s. Thus the majority expected a turning-point around the middle of the 1970s. But a small group of executives thought that in 1982 the climate would still be nationalistic and restrictive, in Sweden as well as abroad.

We have tried to identify the characteristics of the respondents who judged the ethnocentric world to be the most likely. Some of them belonged to fairly large Swedish international companies. They were people who saw no justification in being too optimistic about the future. As one respondent put it: "We have been abroad so long; we've had to survive world wars and depressions, and I hardly think the future will be so very different. The tendencies in the ethnocentric world are nothing new to us, in fact we have learnt to live with them."

Other groups which were more inclined to foresee a restrictive world were top executives in companies whose products were mainly directed towards the home market and companies whose products were regarded as "unique," "special" or "always competitive"—products which had found a niche on the world market from the start.

Thus a common feature among these groups of executives seems to be that as well as regarding a restrictive development as the most probable, they also expect to be able to survive fairly comfortably in such a world. On the other hand, the managers of companies which are just embarking hesitantly upon an internationalization of their businesses, are much more inclined to believe in the geocentric world. They lack the necessary experience for coping with their expansion plans in a restrictive world. Thus we have here another clear manifestation of the tendency to predict the future that one wants and expects to be able to handle. Another sign of this is the tendency that we mentioned above not to "notice" the tentative moves towards the control of international business which are described in the geocentric world.

All the respondents claimed to *prefer* the open, geocentric world, although some of them found it "more risky." In other words they feared that the evolution of the global industrial system might get into the hands of a few giant corporations. This view found some support among the managing directors of subsidiaries of foreign-owned companies. All the business executives in the subsidiaries based in Sweden believed without reservation in the open world. Thus few of them foresaw even a short period of national-ism. The geocentric world was "their" world, and the sooner it was realized the better.

Thus, as a whole, the geocentric development was felt to be much more desirable. Such a world, as one respondent put it, would be "a real feast-day for the big corporations" (although the same executive did not personally want "to live in a world like that thirty years from now").

It is difficult to say whether the business executives see any great difference between Sweden and other countries when it comes to the probability of either of these visions of the future. One group of chief executives, some of them at the head of small companies and others just beginning to locate production abroad, felt that the Swedish trade unions might to some extent work for a more restrictive Sweden. However, these respondents had a rather vague view of conditions abroad, and in answer to direct questions they were generally unable to point to any specific differences. Instead most of them described the Swedish trade union movement as "enlightened," "realistic" and "intelligent" compared with those of other countries (Cf. p. 77 above).

Paradoxically, while the executives were predominantly negative to an internationalization of the trade union movement, they also believed that cooperation with the unions would succeed even in the geocentric world. In other words, they tended to see what they wanted to see—a world friendly to business. Regardless of what the scenario actually suggested, they generally ignored the idea that the open world would almost certainly mean more trade union cooperation over national borders. On the contrary, some of them took it for granted that the trade unions would actually lose part of the power they have at present. A couple of others took the scenario to mean that, as a result of an open attitude on the part of the corporations and because of employee participation in decision-making, the trade unions would gain so much insight into the companies' situation that cooperation would blossom without friction.

Most of the executives believed that the restrictive world would increase the contact between companies and authorities. This would result not in better cooperation but in the opposite: "Everything would be regulated;" "We would have to write hundreds of contracts;" "The more closed in you are, the more rules are needed for governing; unfortunately that happens more or less automatically."

Most of the respondents believed that a coalition government (centre party, liberals and conservatives) would *to some extent* bring us closer to the open world, mainly because of "growing optimism and the spirit of enterprise" rather than because government policy would deviate radically from that of the governing social democrats.

EFFECTS OF THE SCENARIOS ON THE COMPANIES

Markets and Location

What impact would the two alternative futures have on the behavior of the companies? As we can see in Tables 4:5 and 4:6 below, the answers concerning the respondents' own worlds agree fairly well with the answers for the geocentric world. In several cases the figures are exactly the same. We have already suggested that most of those who gave a high probability

Table 4:5

**EFFECTS OF THE SCENARIOS ON INTERNATIONALIZATION:
RELATIVE SIZE OF FOREIGN OPERATIONS IN
ALTERNATIVE SCENARIOS**

	Situation today, 1972	*Forecast for 1982, assuming scenario:*		
		Own World	*Ethnocentric, restrictive*	*Geocentric, supportive*
Proportion of sales abroad (% of total sales)[1]	55	69	54	74
Proportion of production abroad (% of production)[1]	17	31	29	33
Proportion of research and development abroad (% of total R & D)[1]	10	28	18	27

[1] Unweighted mean for the Swedish companies interviewed ($n = 40$).

Table 4:6

**EFFECTS OF THE SCENARIOS ON INTERNATIONALIZATION:
ANNUAL PERCENTAGE INCREASE 1972–82 IN
ALTERNATIVE SCENARIOS**

	Own world	*Ethnocentric, restrictive*	*Geocentric, supportive*
Sales, total at fixed prices[1]	8	5	9
Sales to Swedish customers[1]	4	5	4
Sales to foreign customers[1]	10	5	12
Production in Sweden[1]	6	3	6
Production abroad[1]	12	9	14
Export from Sweden[1]	7	0	8

[1] Unweighted mean for the Swedish companies interviewed ($n = 40$).

rating to the restrictive world were assuming that their own companies' future would be only slightly affected by official actions. This means that the differences here can be attributed mainly to the small and medium-sized companies whose international operations consist of *export* rather than foreign production.

Thus, the geocentric world would mean roughly speaking the same future as the companies "own" world. There would be a slightly higher growth rate and a somewhat more rapid rate of internationalization and specialization, but the differences are not great.

The ethnocentric world produces quite a different picture. In this world the tendency to increase the proportion of sales to foreign markers tails off and the rate of growth is expected to be much lower. This will have an adverse effect chiefly on employment on the home market and on exports. In the ethnocentric world, according to the business executives, the smaller companies would clearly have to develop new products for the home markets instead of continuing to expand abroad within already established product areas. In other words, as one business executive put it, "They would have to go into areas where they don't have the resources to produce efficiently."

The fact that the differences between the expected production shares abroad in the three worlds are nevertheless so small, can be explained as follows. First, in the restrictive world a group of large and internationally established corporations would quickly establish or expand productive units abroad. Secondly, there are some companies which are eager to have the chance to go international, but which may not necessarily exploit this chance in all situations. For them the difference between the scenarios is that in the ethnocentric world they cannot expand abroad but would very much like to do so, while in the geocentric world they can expand but do not have as much motivation to do so. For these companies expansion on foreign markets is thus mainly motivated on defensive grounds.

If we look a little more closely at the figures showing present and expected production abroad, we find four groups or clusters in the distribution of the companies. First, we have the *large international producers* with an average production share abroad of more than 50 percent. Secondly we have a *middle group* with an average of 20 percent of their production abroad. This is followed by a group in the process of expanding abroad—the beginners— which today have only 1 percent or 2 percent of their production abroad but who believe they will have about 20 percent in ten years time. Finally there is a group of companies who have not even considered locating any production abroad at all.

The following table shows the sensitivity of the first three of these groups to the scenarios, as regards production abroad.

Thus the managers of the large Swedish international companies do not seem to expect their companies to be affected at all, as far as the allocation of production is concerned, by developments such as those described in

Table 4:7

	Production abroad (percent of total production)[1]			
	1971	*1982 Own scenario*	*Ethnocentric, restrictive world*	*Geocentric, supportive world*
Swedish MNCs (8)	52	75	75	74
Middle group (10)	20	39	25	42
Beginners (10)	1	21	24	24

[1] Unweighted mean values.

our scenarios. Executives in the middle group, many of whose companies were described as "export companies in the process of going multinational," felt that their business would be more sensitive to a development towards the ethnocentric, restrictive world. These respondents saw the low share of production abroad in the restrictive world as a result of "wanting to, but not being able to." Export companies were said to have to make enormous adjustments before achieving pure MNC status, and many of the respondents stressed that this generally needed "more knowledge and experience than we ever expected to start with."

It also appears from the table that, like the large corporations, the "beginners" would not let themselves be affected by a restrictive world; on the contrary they expected a higher international share in this case than in their "own" world. The beginners explained their expansion plans in a restrictive world with comments such as: "In that kind of world our only chance would be to move out;" "If that's the way it goes, we simply won't be able to stay in Sweden." Establishment abroad in these cases is thus not governed by markets, as in the majority of cases. Instead cost and tax considerations are important. The respondents wanted to move to a more favorable business climate, but they were often not very specific about naming countries where the climate would be better.

In fact some of these executives were more inclined to believe in the ethnocentric than in the geocentric trend and were determined, like most of the others, that their companies would cope even in such a world. In view of the answers and reactions of the group which has already started establishing production abroad, the suspicion that many beginners will find moving abroad much more demanding than they imagine seems to be justified. We cannot exclude the possibility that the answers in these cases may reflect political attitudes rather than carefully considered plans.

As was mentioned above, some saw in the geocentric world a chance to remain in Sweden and yet achieve success, since the disadvantages of the high labor costs on the home market would, it was argued, be less in the open world. This argument also applied by and large to the location of the R & D functions. R & D is transferred abroad, to a considerable extent, in a restrictive world. But the highest level of foreign location for R & D is achieved in the companies' "own" worlds. The geocentric world, on the other hand, makes it possible "to keep R & D at home," with more specialization and a better exploitation of comparative advantages as a result. Also, in the geocentric world the flow of knowledge would be greater both between and within companies.

Organization and Ownership

To judge from the reactions of the respondents, a restrictive scenario would split the companies with subsidiaries abroad into more independent parts. Furthermore, in the ethnocentric world ownership in the foreign subsidiaires would be shared to a greater extent than normally with national stakeholders, in order to comply with the demands for local influence which this scenario implies. We could say that a nationalistic world pushes companies towards polycentric strategies.[1]

The geocentric world, on the other hand, would see more integration of operations. Production would become specialized and duplication of production would be reduced. Control at the strategic level would be strict in this world but, according to the respondents, the subsidiaries would be given considerable independence within fixed limits; they would still identify strongly with the parent company.

A geocentric world would also be accompanied by a rapid international dispersal of ownership in the parent companies. We have already mentioned the causes of this development, and need only point out here that the idea of "selling because we have to" is expected to be less important in a more open world. It is interesting to note that even head-office functions would be relocated to other countries to quite a large extent in a geocentric world.

Sweden's Role in the Scenarios

The corporate executives were also asked about the prospects for Sweden as a nation in the two worlds. All the respondents saw difficulties for Sweden in a restrictive world, mainly because of the country's limited domestic market. According to a few of the executives these difficulties might be offset by the fact that, in a world of this kind, other countries would not have any reason to "fear" Sweden. Instead the big American, Japanese and Western European companies would come under fire; they would be regarded as a greater threat to national sovereignty and self-sufficiency than the companies of "neutral" Sweden.

There were also other indications of a belief in Sweden's comparatively advantageous position in a nationalistic world. The foreign-owned companies were very negative towards the approach to an ethnocentric world, while the Swedish international companies felt they would be able to survive fairly well in a restrictive world: "As Swedes we inspire more confidence;" "We will never be regarded with suspicion;" "As a small (by international standards) company, we can remain more flexible."

Closely related to this attitude is the unwillingness on the part of the heads of Swedish international companies to identify their corporations with their Western European and American "big brothers." Swedish executives are very unwilling to describe their companies as multinationals. This is not because they feel any great mistrust of the giant corporations, but rather because they think it pays to emphasize their own image, as long as the word multinational remains a derogatory term. "We don's want TV debates about us." "We are especially careful about our good public relations, because there's such a lot of ignorant talk about the MNCs."

Finally, the respondents believed that Sweden's advantages in a restrictive world would be lost if Sweden too became restrictive. In their view the best strategy, regardless of what was happening outside the country, would be to adopt an open attitude towards international business.

SUMMARY

The Companies—The Leading Part

The executives' expectations that the internationalization of companies will continue and even accelerate and that a pro-business climate will emerge suggest that most businessmen envisage the company system as the leading part in the internationalization process even in the future. They recognize certain ambitions on the part of the nation states to restrict the process and continue it within narrower bounds, to tighten up the regulations, and to try to exert a more direct influence on developments. At the same time, however, they believe that the politicians will find it extremely difficult to develop effective instruments of control in this sphere. Likewise, many executives are already thinking in terms of defensive adaptive measures: for example, coalitions with other companies and nations, an increase in the relocation of production abroad, more delegation in operational matters in order to create a local image and to adapt operations to local conditions while retaining closer supervision and control of strategic and financial matters.[2]

The internationalization of the trade union movement is regarded in management circles as a very distant prospect. The businessmen do not seem to regret this. Consequently they are not afraid of (or simply do not believe in) a return to protectionism, nationalism and restrictiveness brought on by frustrated trade union hopes; nor do they foresee any big changes in leadership which would give the "grass roots" more direct influence.

Effect of Present Events

The oil crisis of the autumn of 1973 and the winter of 1974 served to remind us again of the sensitivity of long-range forecasts to contemporary events. We had another example of this during the interviews with the business executives, which were held during the period November 1972– March 1973. For instance, during this period a major article appeared in the Swedish daily newspaper *Dagens Nyheter* about support in Japan for the domestic shipbuilding industry. The interviews we held immediately after the appearance of this article contained far more references to the possibility of a nationalistic and restrictive development than the interviews held before. Recent investment decisions in the company concerned, reorganizations, the previous year's results on different markets and so on, certainly affected the answers.

This is interesting from two points of view. First, the attitudes and expectations of major decision-makers are clearly affected by what is going on in the world at the time. This means that long-range commitments are decided under considerable pressure from contemporary happenings in the environment—happenings which may ultimately prove to have been transitory or trivial although they may look at the time like tremendous structural changes. Secondly, apart from the obvious limitations that always apply to any "knowledge" of the future, it means that the method we have used probably does not provide very good forecasts of the future of *individual companies*. Taken as a whole, on the other hand, the net effects of such events as the Japanese article are less serious.

NOTES

1.   Perlmutter (1965) uses the terms ethnocentric, polycentric, and geocentric to describe attitudes in which the home country, the host country, or the world is taken as the base for corporate identity and policy-making.

2. *See* M. R. Brooke and L. H. Remmers (1970) where the authors speak of closed and open relations between group management and subsidiaries as an alternative to the concepts of the centralized and decentralized organization. For example, far-reaching decentralization in operational matters linked with strict central planning and financial control would be described as a closed relation.

5

The Trade Union Movement's Vision of the Future

GENERAL IDEAS ABOUT THE FUTURE

The hopes and expectations of the Swedish trade union movement regarding the future are rather divided. There seems to be a split between the two large central organizations, The Swedish Confederation of Trade Unions (LO) and The Swedish Central Organization of Salaried Employees (TCO), and also between the central and the local levels *within* LO. Despite this, on many important points there is broad agreement throughout the whole trade union movement.

The optimism about the possibility of further economic growth and an increase in welfare in Sweden during the next ten years is very striking. Admittedly, most of the respondents claim that an increasing part of the rise in standard of living will be taken out in the form of more leisure, better working conditions and a gentler pace of life, but prophesies of doom or forecasts of economic stagnation or even recession have no supporters in the Swedish trade union movement. This optimism about Sweden contrasts with a rather dark picture of the future in the developing countries. A certain amount of defeatism seems to have spread on this question; many trade union leaders feel that Sweden has no chance of influencing the situation and, moreover, they envisage strong opposition to aid to the developing countries among the voters and in the local trade union branches. Paradoxically, it is just at the local level that we found people stressing most energetically the necessity of solving the problems of the developing countries, despite the sacrifices that this will demand from the industrialized world. Can it be that politicians and decision-makers in organizations entertain—and spread—a wrong picture of the international support and loyalty of the Swedish people?

In fact international issues occupy a dominating position in the Swedish trade union movement's vision of the future. It is felt that Swedish political life will become increasingly oriented towards international problems, and that even the wage-earner organizations will be forced to devote more time and thought to what happens outside the national borders.

As far as the industrialized world is concerned, the future is expected to bring closer economic and political cooperation between East and West. World trade will increase rapidly, and this is regarded as something positive.

Some, however, fear the pragmatically motivated collaboration between large multinational corporations and the Eastern countries. Integration between Western and Eastern dictatorial power can only lead to a world society in which small units find it difficult to uphold their interests. The trade unions would find such a development regrettable, since it is very difficult to incorporate the eastern countries' trade unions into any international cooperation. But the meeting held in Geneva in January 1974 between representatives of the trade unions of both East and West shows that many people are eager, despite the difficulties, to do everything possible to achieve closer contact with wage-earner organizations in the East. It is suggestive that it was LO's previous chairman, Arne Geijer, who initiated the contacts which resulted in the meeting. Most leading members of the trade union movement expect that Sweden will become more dependent on the Eastern countries for its foreign trade in the future.

The trade union representatives also expect that political and trade union life in Sweden will be concerned mainly with questions of employment, participation in decision-making, and environmental issues. This brings us to one of the points in which opinions in the central organization and in the local trade unions deviate sharply. In the former, it was felt that problems would be solved with a relatively high degree of mutual understanding between the parties concerned, while in the latter it was expected that there would be a sharper polarization in politics and confrontations on the labor market. The differences are illustrated in Table 5:1.

The table shows that there is a clear tendency to predict more polarization in the lower ranks of the LO hierarchy. It seems that the central organizations see it as their task to mediate between deviating interests, to arrive at compromises acceptable by all; also it seems to be felt that the unions' "opponents" on the labor market or in politics will have the same cooperative approach. The difference is somewhat reminiscent of that between the large and small companies with regard to management's view of the authorities. Not to put it too mildly, the small businessmen saw the government departments and other authorities as a crowd of subversive ill-wishers, whereas the heads of the large corporations knew many politicians personally and perhaps saw their political views as a necessary part of their

Table 5:1

DO YOU BELIEVE POLITICAL LIFE IN SWEDEN IN TEN YEARS TIME WILL BE CHARACTERIZED BY A POLARIZATION OR A RAPPROCHEMENT OF OPINIONS, AS COMPARED WITH THE PRESENT?

(number of answers given)			
	Polarization	No Change	Rapprochement
Central LO-organs ($n = 6$)	1	2	3
Union chairmen in LO ($n = 11$)	6	1	4
Shop stewards in LO ($n = 10$)	7	1	2
Central organs in TCO ($n = 6$)	2	1	3

careers. We could say, if we allow ourselves another sweeping generalization, that the "grassroots" in LO look upon the entrepreneurs and their political
representatives as a set of unscrupulous profit-hunters, while the "bigwigs"
see them as men of roughly the same stamp as themselves.

To judge from the interviews, employment will be the great political
and trade union issue during the next ten years. Most trade union leaders
predict enormous problems due to a structural decline in industrial employment. The solutions which they envisage involve creating job opportunities
in the service industries, in particular in the public sector. They also predict
that "society" will intervene increasingly and more directly in other parts
of the economy. Traditional economic-political measures will not be sufficient
to solve the problems of adjustment; a more active role on the part of society
will be necessary. At the central level of LO it is held that the enormous
capital requirements of future investments alone will call for a contribution
on the part of "society." Furthermore, it is claimed, the increasing concentration and ever more rapid internationalization of the economy mean that
industry, and other branches of the economy as well, will be subjected to a
greater measure of social control and regulation. It is worth noting that
almost all those who predicted an increase in social control over the economy
were opposed to the idea of the state administering and exercising all
power. Instead, they prefer the planning of the economy to be undertaken
in consultation between "all the parties concerned," i.e., the state, the
trade unions, and representatives of industry.

At the top of LO, moreoever, there is a very low opinion of the Riksdag's
possibilities of influencing economic life. Instead, economic development is
claimed to be controlled by the parties on the labor market and, to some
extent, by a small group of ministers. "When an industrial magnate has
something on his mind, he doesn't go to the Swedish Riksdag but to the
Minister of Finance." In the higher ranks of the hierarchy this idea about
consultation at the central level is very marked, while at the local and sometimes also at the branch level, ideas run more towards direct control on the
part of the state and the wage-earner organizations.

Also, when it comes to the introduction of more democracy into
working life, expectations at the local level and, perhaps surprisingly, within
TCO, are higher than at the central LO level and among the union chairmen.
The latter, for example, regard the utilization of the state pension funds as
an injection of capital into Swedish industry which is facing harsh foreign
competition, while at the local level the pension funds are seen as a possible
way of ensuring "society's" control over the actions and activities of the
business corporations.

It is clear that the Swedish trade union movement is prepared for a
decline in industrial employment. The branches of industry which appear
to have a future are said to be those based on domestic supply of raw
materials and the technology-intensive parts of industry. We can, therefore,
expect that a decline in employment in these industries too would be
regarded with considerable anxiety.

On all levels in the Swedish trade union movement an extension of the
tasks undertaken by the wage-earner organizations is expected. Issues such

as environmental pollution, industrial democracy, and employment policy will all demand more time and resources. Insofar as this means penetrating into areas traditionally belonging to general politics, a change in work forms is also probable. The classical way of fighting for wage-earner interests, i.e., through bargaining with the employers and initiating strike action against them if the results of the bargaining are meagre, will in many areas have to give way to attempts to satisfy the interests of the members through legislation, by collaboration with the Riksdag and the government. It is not expected that LO's traditional relationship with the social democratic party will change within the next ten years, but in TCO particularly there is some uncertainty as to how things will develop over a slightly longer period. It is claimed that the stagnation in industrial employment together with the efforts towards cooperation between different wage-earner organizations may serve to promote a divorce between trade union organizations and political parties. On the other hand, people in LO expect that TCO and the other salaried-workers' organizations will become more politically aware, and that trade union co-operation will not threaten the alliance between the trade unions and the political part of the labor movement.

THE TRADE UNION MOVEMENT AND THE INTERNATIONALIZATION OF INDUSTRY

The internationalization of industry has been increasingly the focus of attention in recent years in the trade union organizations. The clearest expression of this interest is the report of the Swedish Metal Workers' Union on the multinational corporations, which was discussed at the Union's Congress in the Autumn of 1973.[1] Our interviews confirm the impression that the question of the international mobility of capital occupies a prominent place in the Swedish trade union movement's thinking about the future. The discussion often turned spontaneously to the problem of the MNCs even before we had revealed that this was our chief interest. One of the most awkward stumbling-blocks for the researcher is the question of the relevance of his area of interest to the people who are expected to increase his information about it. If the relevance is poor, if the interviewee is not particularly interested in the problems discussed during the interview, the validity of the questions is also likely to be poor, i.e., it will be difficult for the researcher to decide what exactly the respondent is answering. In the present case this risk is probably slight. The majority of the respondents were obviously stimulated by the discussions and considered our questions extremely important.

What, then, were the expectations of the trade union movement regarding Swedish industry's future foreign commitments and the operations of foreign companies in Sweden? In Table 5:2 some of the "forecasts" we asked our respondents to draw up are summarized.

As we can see from this table, there is no forecast of any cessation in internationalization. On the contrary, everyone without exception is prepared for an increase in international enterprise. Nevertheless, the figures are

Table 5:2

	The situation today	LO's forecast[2] for 1983	TCO's forecast[3] for 1983
Proportion of sales abroad for Swedish industrial companies (% of total sales)	55%[1]	65%	63%
Proportion of production abroad for Swedish industrial companies (% of total production)	17%[1]	23%	22%
Proportion employed in foreign-owned industry in Sweden (% of total employed in industry)	10%	13%	11%
Growth in the production of Swedish-owned companies up to 1984 (% per year)	5%/year[4]	5.8%/year	5.5%/year

[1] Unweighted mean for the Swedish companies interviewed in 1972 ($n = 40$).
[2] Mean value of all respondents ($n = 25$).
[3] Mean value of all respondents ($n = 6$).
[4] Rough average for the period 1960–1970.
The figures in the first column were given to the respondent in the interview.

much lower than in the corresponding forecast of the company executives. In Chapter 7 we will look a little more closely at these differences and their probable implications for future events.

Opinions also differ in the trade unions about the probable future appearance of international business. The general tendency is that people in the central LO organs predict a more rapid rate of internationalization than those at "lower" levels in LO. This probably depends partly on the fact that the trade union officials at the local level do not have as much access as the people at the top to information about the latest developments and company plans. It is obvious that the people at the local level would be surprised, to put it mildly, if the plans of the business leaders ever came to fruition. When the shop stewards were confronted with the employers' expectations of the future, their reactions were often expressed in terms such as: "Quite unrealistic, but it's understandable that they put it like this; they're always optimists except when it comes to wage talks;" "We know what to expect of them;" "They are overestimating the opportunities for growth abroad." It was clearly difficult for the trade union representatives, and particularly those at the local level, to believe the figures we gave them. The figures were understood as an expression of professional optimism on the part of the executives rather than as descriptions of probable and attainable future states. If this view should turn out to be wrong, it is easy to imagine strong reactions on the part of the trade union movement when the "information gap" is bridged.

However, lack of information about company plans is not the only

Table 5:3

**"HOW WOULD YOU DESCRIBE SWEDISH POLICY
TODAY, AND WHAT DO YOU THINK IT WILL BE
LIKE IN TEN YEARS TIME IN THE FOLLOWING AREAS ...?"**

(Scale 1–5; 1 = very liberal; 5 = very restrictive)

	The situation[1] today according to LO (n = 25)	In 10 years[1] according to LO (n = 25)	The situation[1] today according to the executives (n = 40)	In 10 years[1] according to the executives (n = 40)
Trade policy	1.7	1.5	2.2	2.1
Policy towards the investments of Swedish companies in other countries	1.6	2.7	3.0	2.9
Policy towards the investments of foreign companies in Sweden	1.6	2.7	2.6	2.5
Policy towards the immigration and emigration of labor	2.6	3.4	2.8	2.9

[1] Mean values for all respondents.

factor behind the different expected rates of internationalization. The company executives and the trade union leaders also diverge when it comes to their views of future public policy vis-à-vis the companies' foreign commitments. In Table 5:3 we have summarized LO's and the business executives' forecasts of policies towards international business.

It is immediately striking that the business executives regard Sweden's present policy as much more restrictive than the LO representatives do. More interesting, however, is that the two sides diverge in their view of future developments. LO expects the policy to become much more restrictive, while the executives imagine that the status quo will be more or less maintained. Thus it is probable that differences in the tate of internationalization forecast for Swedish industry depend at least in part on different expectations about the way legislation will develop in that area. This interpretation of results is supported by the trade union leaders' estimations of the effects of Scenario A, the liberal scenario. Given an environment that is more like that of the business executives, LO revises its forecast upwards both as regards sales and production abroad (*see* p. 100).

Control of International Business

Thus, in the Swedish trade union movement, a tightening up of the restrictions on international business is both desired and believed to be within reach. This is not to be confused with a nationalistic and protectionist attitude. Instead, the view is that internationalization in itself has many advantages: production can be managed more rationally; Swedish companies can acquire export markets by establishing production abroad; foreign companies can provide employment in Sweden, they can introduce technical know-how and facilitate international contacts and collaboration over frontiers, which is a good thing in itself. The danger lies, it is felt, in the fact that by organizing themselves across national boundaries the companies may achieve too much power, thus becoming inaccessible to national political measures and trade union action. The companies cannot be expected to take other than commercial and economic considerations into account in locating their production or in distributing their profits between countries etc., which makes it necessary to exercise strict social control over the internationally operating companies. This can be effected in a variety of ways.

It is expected that *Swedish companies will be subject to stricter scrutiny as regards the socio-economic consequences of foreign investments.* In particular employment aspects will be considered. Many trade union leaders have reacted strongly against foreign establishments undertaken with a view to acquiring cheap foreign labor in countries such as Portugal, Finland, and the Latin American countries. But if the reasons for launching operations in other countries lie instead in such factors as high transport costs or proximity to the local market, their attitude is considerably more positive. As regards the forms that stricter control should assume, there is considerable uncertainty. However, it is clear that some form of *testing of individual cases* is required; also, the views of the wage-earner organizations should carry great weight when decisions are being taken. Other possible ways of exercising control include an increase in industrial democracy and an extension of direct state or union ownership in companies. In this context the local unions attach great hopes to the pension funds, while at the central level these funds are regarded rather as a source of financing available to all types of Swedish companies, including MNCs. From an extension of industrial democracy the wage-earners hope in the first place to acquire greater insight into the actions and activities of the internationally operating companies. The lack of information about investment plans is regarded by many as a major threat to the interests of the wage earners and the national economy.

More *supervision of the operations of foreign companies in Sweden* is called for. The opportunities for tax evasion enjoyed by these companies are regarded as a problem, but even more important to many influential trade union leaders is the danger that Swedish-owned companies will be purchased by foreign interests and subsequently closed down. Examples in the shoe industry have caused anxiety to many people. In this sphere greater efforts on the part of the government to retain ownership within the borders are seen as a necessity, and state take-overs of companies threatened with purchase are seen as one possibility. Moreover, the trade unions intend to make great effort to get better insight into the operations of the foreign companies. Some of the large foreign MNCs in Sweden have pursued an anti-trade-union policy, which has hitherto made them inaccessible to pressure. It is quite clear that these companies are the ones which will be subjected to the strictest measures.

Internationally agreed regulation of the multinational corporations is desired, but there is obviously no very great belief in the likelihood of such a development. At top levels in the central organizations, particularly, there is a pessimistic view of the possibility of getting anything effective done in bodies such as the United Nations and OECD. Instead, it is felt that when it comes to legislation against MNCs the work will have to be done at the national level. However, this does not mean that laws will be passed independently of foreign interests; the Swedish trade union movement at least would not participate in any such action.

Strong *international trade union co-operation* is regarded as essential. Up to now Sweden has played a leading role in this respect, and it does not seem particularly likely that other countries will show as much enthusiasm in this area in future as Sweden has traditionally shown. This applies particularly to cooperation between the central organs. The political and religious divisions, and the variety of conditions for the exercise of power at the national level which characterize the international trade union movement, make any effective institutionalized collaboration at the central level very unlikely. For example, none of our respondents believed in international collective bargaining within the foreseeable future. On the other hand, the chances of achieving strong international links within individual trade unions were regarded as considerably better. In particular, there was confidence— and not only in the unions concerned—in the ability of the metal workers', the engineering workers' and the building workers' internationals to establish an internationally organized counterweight to the MNCs in the reasonably near future.

Another model for trade union strategy consists of internationally coordinated action within individual companies. It is at the local level that conditions for an awareness on the part of the wage earners in different countries regarding their common interest vis-à-vis the multinational employers are most favorable, and the problem of initiating trade union action is the least complicated organizationally. The kinds of action which come to mind range from the simple exchange of information about different parts of the same company, over intra-company coordinated strike action to satisfy the demands of wage earners in separate countries, to coordinated wage bargaining. The advantage of this type of trade union cooperation is the speed of action that it allows and its adaptability to conditions in the individual companies. The main disadvantage is the lack of coordination in strong central organs and, an extension of this, the threat to the whole of the established hierarchical trade union model that strong decentralized trade union activity represents. Further, it is well known that many large multinational corporations would like nothing better than to see the wage-earners organize themselves company-wise.

All this shows very clearly that the Swedish trade union movement is *not* negative in its attitude to internationalized industry as such. Given control by society over the internationally operating companies, Swedish or foreign, an increase in international specialization is to be desired. In the Swedish wage-earner organizations there is a strong tradition in favor of free trade and a positive attitude to international contacts in general, that lacks an equivalent in most other parts of the world. In the the local unions, too, this principle is stressed very strongly. On the other hand, what cannot be tolerated is any tendency for industry to develop a superstructure above all national institutions and inaccessible to political and trade union action. What causes anxiety in the first instance is the gap between company profit and social benefit in connection with employment, the raw materials supply situation, taxation, etc.; in the longer run there is also anxiety about the possible undermining of the whole Western democratic system.

This ambivalence between a generally favourable attitude to internationalization and a fear of its consequences in a world where internationalism is administered by privately owned companies, has its equivalent in the view of the political and trade union strategies that are available. The most attractive solution is said to be a combination of internationally agreed legislation and trade union activity at an international level. This is the path which LO and TCO would really prefer to follow, but they also foresee enormous difficulties which modify these ambitions and make other geographically more limited and possibly more restrictive models relevant. "*If* we can't achieve a functioning international system for general planning, then we will have to turn to more direct national types of control over the corporations' foreign activities." This is roughly the substance of the majority view. It is important to note that even according to this view no significant reduction in the international dependence of Swedish industry is envisaged. "One in every three members of LO is involved in the production of goods for export." "We live on our foreign trade." "A small country like Swedish can never close its frontiers." All these comments reflect the same view of Sweden's place in the global system. It is also significant that in the geocentric and regulatory scenario, which is favored by the unions and which represents a genuinely internationalistic world, the rate of internationalization predicted is *higher* than the rate that would be expected under more normal conditions (*see* p. 100).

It may be difficult to conceive the real gap that distinguishes a Swedish trade union man from, for example, his American counterpart. Our American sister study provides substantial confirmation of this. The internationalism and free-trade thinking that Sweden has inherited from the social democratic movement have no equivalents in the isolatistminded USA. Furthermore, many Swedish trade union leaders feel responsibility not only for the wage situation of their own members but for Swedish society as a whole.

This, which Roland Huntford in his book *The New Totalitarians*[2] sees as corporativism and complacence, is part of the explanation of the "balanced" view of the problems of internationalization that prevails in Sweden. Reactions to the ethnocentric Scenario B provide a good illustration of the Swedish trade union movement's negative attitude towards protectionism. This scenario was regarded by most of our respondents as *worse* than the laissez faire Scenario A; it was claimed to lead to a much lower rate of economic growth and was rejected for reflecting a parochial approach

Table 5:4

"HOW WOULD YOU DESCRIBE PRESENT SWEDISH POLICY AND WHAT DO YOU THINK IT WILL BE LIKE IN TEN YEARS TIME IN THE FOLLOWING AREAS ... ?"

(Scale 1–5; 1 = very liberal; 5 = very restrictive)

	Trade policy		Policy towards the investments of Swedish companies in other countries		Policy towards foreign investments in Sweden	
	Today	In 10 years time	Today	In 10 years time	Today	In 10 years time
Central LO-organs[1] (n = 5)	1.2	1.2	1.2	2.2	1.2	1.6
Trade union leaders in LO (n = 11)	1.5	1.5	1.6	2.8	1.5	2.6
Shop stewards in LO[1] (n = 9)	2.1	1.8	1.8	2.8	1.9	3.3
Central and union organs in TCO[1] (n = 6)	1.7	1.7	1.8	2.0	2.0	2.2
Company executives[1] (n = 40)	2.3	2.1	3.0	3.0	2.6	2.5

[1] Mean values for all respondents.

and failing to provide opportunities for individual people and for industry as a whole. This firm rejection as a matter of principle had no equivalent in the reactions of the American trade unions. Their attitude was much more "materialistic;" they asked themselves how protectionism could be exploited as a weapon in the struggle for short-run economic advantages for the unions and their members. In Chapter 7 we will discuss in more detail the implications for Sweden of this tendency on the part of the large nations to pursue an ethnocentric nationalistic policy, from which they are also more likely to be able to benefit.

Differences within the Swedish Trade Union Movement

Of course opinions also differ within the Swedish trade union movement about what futures are desirable and probable. We have already mentioned that expectations about the rate of industrial internationalization are more modest at lower levels in LO than they are in the central organs. There are also interesting differences in opinions about future legislation. To illustrate some of these we have divided the results presented in Table 5:3 into the categories shown in Table 5:4.

The first thing we notice here is the big differences in the assessments of the present situation. From the methodological point of view this involves an awkward problem of interpretation, since it is uncertain what basis for comparison the respondents have used. Is it the situation ten years ago, or the "ideal" state, or the policy in other countries, or something else altogether? On the other hand, we can be fairly sure that comparisons between intra-group perceptions of *changes* are methodologically defensible. On this basis, the conclusions to be drawn from Table 5:4 are, first, that there is a great difference between LO and the business executives when it comes to forecasting policy on the flow of investment over national boundaries in general; secondly, there is also a big difference between LO and TCO on this same question; thirdly, opinions differ within LO about future policy on foreign investment in Sweden.

The attitude of TCO (the Central Organization of Salaried Employees) to the problem of internationalization can be explained in part by the fact that developments have not yet directly affected its members to any great extent. Since employment is the overriding consideration in determining a union's attitude to questions of investment, and since companies have so far only had to choose between domestic or foreign locations in the case of production alone, TCO's relatively liberal attitude is understandable. However, many TCO representatives expressed some anxiety over several recent cases of transferring administrative and research work abroad. SKF's establishment of an international research centre in the Netherlands was mentioned on several occasions as a manifestation of a disquieting tendency. In light of general company plans for a rapid internationalization of research and development work (*see* Chapter 4), there is reason to believe that TCO will also engage itself more directly in these questions from now on. Obviously their thinking at present is influenced by a general liberal view of international questions rather than by any consideration of specific cases. For this reason it seems probable that the views of the two large wage-earner organizations will tend to converge despite the different political affiliations of their leaders.

The division within LO is thus mainly connected with differing views on foreign companies. The top management of LO welcomes them as bearers of employment and transmitters of know-how, while the local unions are afraid of their power to disregard trade union action and to close down or move production as it suits them. There is also some disagreement about the foreign operations of Swedish companies. In this case, however, it is mainly a question of the *forms* which the necessary social control should assume The trade union leadership envisages further expansion of general control mechanisms combined with some form of tripartite organ (companies, government, and trade union movement) to scrutinize individual cases and, in a spirit of mutual understanding, to agree on decisions acceptable from the national economic point of view. At the local level there is considerably more "regulatory" thinking, i.e., a desire for more specific and direct control of foreign investments on the part of the authorities and the trade unions. Furthermore, the local bodies want to give more weight to local wage-earner interests (rather than national economic interests) when decisions are being made.

Table 5:5

PROBABILITY OF SCENARIOS A, B AND C

(Scale 1–5; 1 = very improbable; 5 = very probable)

	Scenario A (liberal)	Scenario B (ethnocentric)	Scenario C (regulatory)
Central LO organs (n = 5)[1]	3.4	2.0	2.0
Union chairmen in LO (n = 11)[1]	2.6	2.1	2.9
Shop stewards in LO (n = 9)[1]	2.4	2.6	3.4
Central and union organs in TCO (n = 6)	3.8	1.0	2.7

[1] Mean values for all respondents.

THE TRADE UNION MOVEMENT ON THE SCENARIOS

Probability and Desirability

Our discussion of the scenarios provided interesting proof of the different futures envisaged within the Swedish trade union movement. In Table 5:5 we have summarized the probability ratings of the scenarios.

As can be seen, there is a general trend in the higher ranks of the LO hierarchy to regard a development of the laissez-faire type (Scenario A) as more probable, and a protectionistic regulatory development as less probable than is the case in the lower ranks. Scenario C, the internationalistic regulatory solution, was regarded in the central LO organs as a utopia, a beautiful but unrealizable dream. Doubt was expressed about the desirability of "unbridled capitalism" as described in Scenario A, although at the same time this development was regarded as relatively probable.

When we look at the respondents' views about desirable futures (Table 5:6), we find that an even more interesting pattern emerges.

The desirability of Scenario A rises monotonously and that of Scenario B

Table 5:6

DESIRABILITY OF SCENARIOS A, B AND C

(Scale 1–5; 1 = not at all desirable; 5 = very desirable)

	Scenario A (liberal)	Scenario B (ethnocentric)	Scenario C (regulatory)
Central LO organs (n = 5)[1]	3.6	1.6	4.4
Union chairmen in LO (n = 11)[1]	3.0	1.9	4.2
Shop stewards in LO (n = 9)[1]	1.9	2.3	4.4
TCO (n = 6)	4.3	1.0	4.2

[1] Mean values for all respondents.

declines monotonously, the higher we go in the LO hierarchy. Scenario C is the only one commanding agreement in all groups, including TCO. As we have seen above, however, this Scenario is regarded as something of a utopia by the top people in LO and TCO, and there is, therefore, reason to look a little more closely at the opinions expressed about the other two scenarios. We will return to the role of Scenario C as a synthesis of internationalism and national interests in Chapter 7. Let us take the scenarios in alphabetical order: Scenario A is regarded as a pretty bright future at the central level in LO, as a moderately desirable development among the unions, and as an intolerable manifestation of unbridled capitalism at the shop-floor level. If this last level were to suspect that developments actually were moving towards a state similar to that described in this scenario, i.e., a gradual liberalizing of the rules for international capital flow, and if at the same time it was felt that this development found some support among the top ranks of the labor movement, then it is easy to imagine an outbreak of serious internal conflict. But the local wage-earners' representatives base their negative view of Scenario A on the supposition that severe economic difficulties—in particular unemployment—would be an inevitable consequence in Sweden of this type of world. The top ranks in LO, on the other hand, have a brighter picture of the effects of Scenario A on the Swedish economy. Thus it could perhaps be argued, if the purely ideological aspects of the scenario are disregarded and only its more everyday implications considered, that the risk of internal conflict would probably disappear automatically as the future was actually realized and new information became available. However, whenever employment problems became acute, the tendency to blame the problems on the internationalization of business would be much greater at the local than at the central level. This, added to the fact that it is difficult to determine the causal relationship between employment and foreign investment "objectively," makes it likely that pressure will be felt from the lower ranks in favor of a strict attitude towards the international corporations regardless of the "true" situation.[3]

Furthermore, there is obviously pressure from below of a more fundamental and ideological kind. At the local level the world is regarded with more radical eyes, and restrictions on the opportunities for trade union and political action are less readily accepted. Time and time again people at the central level in LO said "we are realists," and this led them to make forecasts more cautious than any that could ever be considered at the local level. Many members of TCO appear to appreciate and align themselves with this realistic LO approach. We also have to remember the strong liberal tradition (in the economic sense) of the LO leadership. In particular LO's economic experts have declared their solid support for ideas such as free trade, competition in industry, and economic efficiency. These principles are not upheld as strongly in the lower ranks.

The reactions to Scenario B provide further support for these arguments. Tolerance of protectionistic measures is greater at the local than at the central level in LO; nor should we overlook the extremely negative attitude of TCO towards this ethnocentric scenario. It should be noted, however, that all the respondents nevertheless agree that scenario B as a whole is not a particularly desirable state. Even the shop stewards are strongly opposed to the nationalistic aspects of the scenario. However, they feel that Sweden might be *compelled* to impose measures similar to those described in the scenario if foreign dominance in industry and the unchecked location of Swedish-owned companies abroad assumed threatening proportions.

The idea of "having to" take various steps recurred frequently in the comments on Scenario B at the local level; the Swedish trade unions would not initiate a development towards protectionism unless they felt provoked to do so. Furthermore, several of the respondents declared that the scenario sounded too negative: Sweden could well behave in the way prescribed in the scenario without this leading to such negative effects on the world in general as those described. In fact, for several shop stewards, the step from Scenario B to Scenario C did not seem particularly great. In the same way respondents who did not really object to Scenario A said that its picture of the world was not so far from that of Scenario C, which could well represent a development of A at a later stage in the future. To make a wild generalization, we could perhaps say that people agreed on the goal— Scenario C. But they disagreed about the route—whether it should proceed from Scenario A or Scenario B. This is all the more remarkable since Scenario C certainly cannot be described as a diffuse or shapeless vision of the future; it embraces some very specific elements, including a substantial increase in aid to developing countries, the fragmentation of the multinational corporations, and new organizational frameworks for the administration of international industrial collaboration.

EFFECTS OF THE SCENARIOS ON
SWEDISH INDUSTRY

The forecasts about the future internationalization of Swedish industry, under alternative assumptions about its environment as expressed in our scenarios, illustrate very clearly how these scenarios were interpreted in the different parts of the trade union movement.

Table 5:7 illustrates many interesting relations. First, LO sees Scenario A as involving an increase in the rate of internationalization, which supports our explanation of the differences in the forecasts described apove (p. 92). In other words, it is not likely that lack of information alone accounts for LO's more modest forecasts; the value judgments regarding the process of internationalization as such also come into the picture. Secondly, to Swedish trade union officials Scenario C represents an internationalist world rather than a policy against all international business. Thirdly, Scenario B is regarded by the wage-earners' representatives and by the business executives as a world hostile to growth. Since the business leaders' results consist of "forecasts" aggregated from data referring to the individual companies, we cannot make any direct comparisons between the way in which LO and the executives evaluated the *absolute size* of growth. On the other hand, it should be possible to compare the *relative* rates of growth predicted by the different groups for the alternative scenarios. Fourthly, and this we regard as the most important point, the *business executives*

Table 5:7

	The situation today	In 10 years time	Scenario A (liberal)	Scenario B (ethnocentric)	Scenario C (regulatory)
Proportion of sales abroad for Swedish industrial companies (percent of total sales)					
LO[1]	55[2]	65	67	52	66
Business executives[3]	55	69	69	54	—
Proportion of production abroad for Swedish industrial companies (percent of total production)					
LO[1]	17[2]	23	27	18	24
Business executives[3]	17	31	31	29	—
Proportion employed in industry in foreign-owned industry in Sweden (percent of total employed in industry)					
LO[1]	10	13	15	10	14
Business executives[3]	—	—	—	—	—
Growth in the production of Swedish-owned companies during the next ten years (percent per year)					
LO[1]	5.0[4]	5.8	5.9	4.1	5.6
Business executives[3]	5.0	8.0	8.0	5.0	—

[1] Mean value for all respondents.
[2] Mean value for the Swedish companies interviewed in 1972.
[3] Mean value of evaluations by the business executives of their own company's future.
[4] Average for the years 1960–1970.

and the LO representatives have totally different views about the effects of a restrictive policy on the foreign investments of Swedish companies. While the former regard Scenario B as an ineffective strategy for limiting the growth of production on foreign markets, the trade union leaders believe that this scenario would go a long way towards stopping the "drain" of production from Sweden. When we explained to the trade union leaders how the executives had motivated their estimates, the reaction was: "They underestimate us;" "They think they can pull anything off;" "Nothing but arguments;" "That just shows how much social responsibility they have, but they'll never be able to do it." Naturally the attraction of the ethnocentric Scenario B increases insofar as one believes its inherent policy to be efficient, albeit from limited viewpoints. For this reason, and despite a certain amount of opposition as a matter of principle, we should not altogether exclude the possibility of a restrictive and, in a dynamic perspective, protectionist trade union policy.

SUMMARY

To summarize, we could say that the future behavior of the Swedish trade union movement with regard to the internationally operating companies depends, to a great extent, on factors outside the unions' control. *If* international trade union cooperation increases in strength, *if* supranational political organs succeed in creating frameworks for the operations of the multinational corporations, and *if* the wage-earners' organizations in Sweden are ensured full access to information in the companies and some influence on foreign investment decisions, then the trade union movement will be positive in its attitude to the further internationalization of industry. If, on the other hand, it proves impossible to involve major foreign wage-earner organizations in trade union collaboration across the frontiers; if UN, OECD and similar organizations are not able to produce uniform rules; and if wage-earner interests are not represented when the companies make their investment decisions, then there will be no alternative to a series of separate measures to attain short-term goals, sometimes by rough-and-ready means, and all aimed at preventing rather than controlling the internationalization of business. There would be much more likelihood of this kind of development during periods of unemployment, when the opinions of the rank and file in LO would weigh more heavily. Further, any unscrupulous exploitation by the companies of the difficulties attendant on creating international control systems, or any exploitation of the always possible loopholes in investment regulations, would substantially increase risk of a relapse into ethnocentrism and protectionism.

NOTES

1. *See* "Rapport om Multinationella Företag," *Svenska Metallindustriarbetareförbundet,* 1973.
2. R. Huntford, *The New Totalitarians.* London: The Penguin Press, 1971.
3. In Chapter 7 (pp. 123–50 below) we discuss in greater detail the possible effects that the difficulty of measuring the "consequences" of the internationalization process may have on trade union and political action in the future.

6

The Politicians' Vision of the Future

THE POLITICIANS—A HOMOGENEOUS GROUP?

A politician's job is to represent the views of the electorate, and the aim of the democratic parliamentary system is to see that a variety of ideas are represented among the politicians leading the country. For this reason one can expect that assessments, evaluations and plans about the future of Sweden will vary much more in the political system than in the company or trade union systems. The last two systems can be said to represent relatively clear-cut and partial interests, in a way that the political system does not. Nevertheless, on questions concerning global economic inter-dependencies we found a remarkable degree of unity among politicians of different shades. We are clearly justified, as we will later hope to show, in identifying business as the leading part in the internationalization process. There is much less diversity in the expectations of officials of different political loyalties in the various authorities than there is between the political group as a whole and the business executive group. Before taking a closer look at the question of internationalization, however, a few more general points should be mentioned.

Foreign observers of Swedish political life are often surprised at the calm atmosphere and the apparent absence of major differences of opinion between the major parties. These onlookers are often a little sarcastic about the great interest that really quite trivial differences can arouse in the course of Swedish political debate. A comparison of our interview results with the state of affairs internationally does confirm the idea of Sweden as rather a tranquil place. It was often stressed during the interviews that all the political parties agreed on fundamental issues, that much the same policy would be pursued regardless of which party was in power, or that existing differences of opinion represented nothing more than different shades of generally accepted views. The equivalent among the politicians to the basic "Saltsjöbaden agreement" between the parties on the labor market is an awareness or a basic community of interests across party frontiers.[1] Because of the general acceptance of political activity as a profession rather than a call, the members of the four major parties can regard their opponents in the political arena as colleagues whose problems are similar to their own and whose interests, by and large, they share. Conservative politicians, for example, often mentioned the allowances made by the social democratic

103

government for temporary shifts in opinion among the electorate; they admitted that this was probably necessary and that they often had to make the same sort of allowances themselves.

This idea that the problem of all politicians is to explain their behavior and justify their existence to "the people" is reflected in the way the politicians look upon other power clusters in society. In comparison with the trade union movement, and particularly with the local levels, the politicians as a group have very much more faith in the unanimity between the interests of various partial groups and those of society as a whole. Businessmen were often praised for the valuable contribution they make, and the idea of conflict between capital and labour perceived at the lower levels of LO did not at all meet with the same approval among, for example, social democratic members of the Riksdag. To a greater extent even than the central officials in LO, the politicians see themselves as standing *above* narrow partial interests, rather than as representing them. We also found that the closer a person comes to the centres of power—both inside the individual parties and on the traditional scale from political left to political right—the more respect he feels for his political and other opponents. We found the same difference when it came to assessing opponents between the heads of large companies and the small businessmen. To put it briefly, the *élite in Sweden is very homogeneous*. This could affect the future in two ways, each of them pulling in opposite directions. First, the chances of reaching agreement between decision-makers at a high level in different camps should be good. Secondly, there is a real risk that the latent tensions *within* established social subsystems may be triggered off, just because the lower ranks and local interest groups suspect the upper echelons of "too much" willingness to compromise and collaborate.

In the political system and the trade union system, higher officials tend to envisage more restrictions on the possible future actions of the trade unions, the parties, etc., than the rank-and-file generally expect. For instance, among the "ordinary" social democratic members of the Riksdag, there is a very much stronger belief in the possibility of steering and planning the future than there is among members of the government and experts in the government departments. In view of restrictions from other countries, and out of respect for "justified interests" within the country, the latter are generally prepared to make only very cautious prophesies about basic shifts in power and to speak more fatalistically about the future, which they see as being decided to a great extent by circumstances over which we have no control. Prime Minister Palme's proverb, "Politics is to will," is received with much greater appreciation at the grass-roots level in the labor movement than it is among his fellow ministers.

Politicians in the opposition parties see even less chance than the most "realistic" of the social democrats of steering the future of the world or of Sweden by means of political decisions. In their view the consequences of going against the stream or the "trend" can be unfortunate; a small country like Sweden in particular has no weight to put on the scales that decide the future. Part of the explanation of this difference probably lies in a belief in the workings of the market forces, the liberal economic doctrine that dominates the ideological background of the liberal-conservative opposition. Another explanation may be that the opposition's long absence from power has undermined the faith of the liberal and conservative politicians in the possibilities of political action; they have spent too long making recommendations without any result in practical measures or social changes. It is interesting to note that the tendency for forecasts to agree with hopes also declines as we move from left to right among ordinary Swedish citizens. A survey of the Swedish people's expectations for the future was carried out by the business weekly *Veckans Affärer* together with the Swedish Institute for Public Opinion Research in connection with the "Futures of Sweden" research project, and thus also showed that the conservative and liberal voters were more apathetic and felt more powerless to influence developments than those who voted for the social democrats.[2]

In the previous chapter we saw that the Swedish trade union movement was fairly optimistic about the growth of production in Swedish industry. The politicians predict a slightly slower rate of growth than during the 1960s. It is perhaps rather surprising that the "ordinary" members of parliament envisage the greatest decline; they are also most prepared to accept a lower rate of expansion in the economy in general. One of the restraints on the future action of their respective organizations envisaged by experts and top officials in the trade unions and the political parties, is the shortsightedness of the rank-and-file, who are expected to look no further than their own wage packets and to vote at elections accordingly. Although the views of the rank-and-file of the Swedish people are certainly not represented by the politicians and probably not by the shop stewards either, the results of this study nevertheless suggest that the "establishment" exaggerates—and, therefore, in the long run perhaps even provokes the crassly egotistical money-oriented attitude among the people who put the decision-makers in power.

THE POLITICIANS ON THE
INTERNATIONALIZATION OF INDUSTRY

Like the trade union leaders, the politicians expect the expansion of international business to continue. In fact on this point the forecasts of these two systems agree very closely, while the business executives predict a much higher rate. Some of our respondents' attempts at prophesy are presented in Table 6:1 below. The results seem to confirm the hypothesis that in comparison with the business system the political institutions and the wage-earner organizations represent "lagging" systems. We find that the views of the leading system's own administrators about their system's future behaviour diverge from the views of those who have been appointed to protect the interests of other groups. It seems reasonable to suppose that these differences may contain the seed of future confrontations, when the gap no longer concerns expectations only but refers to the difference between plans and actual outcomes. When the executives' forecasts were presented to the politicians, the response was: "We won't agree to that;" "Far too much;" "We'll have to clamp down on that" and similar remarks. This

Table 6:1

	The situation today	The politicians' forecast for 1983[2]	LO's forecast[3]	Business executives' forecast[3]
Proportion of sales abroad for Swedish manufacturing companies (percent of total sales)	55[1]	63	65	69
Proportion of production abroad for Swedish manufacturing companies (percent of total production)	17[1]	24	23	31
Proportion of industrial employees in foreign-owned industry in Sweden (percent of total industrial employment)	10	16	13	—
Growth in Swedish manufacturing companies' production over the next 10 years (percent per year)	5.0[4]	4.7	5.8	8.0

[1] Unweighted mean value for the Swedish companies interviewed in 1972 ($n = 40$).
[2] Mean value for all respondents ($n = 26$).
[3] Unweighted mean value of evaluations by the business executives of their *own* company's future ($n = 40$).
[4] Approximate mean value for the period 1960–1970.

reaction referred to the proportion of production located abroad and, perhaps even more clearly, to the executives prediction about the rapid internationalization of research and development activities.

An obvious reaction to the above argument is to question the homogeneity of the political group. Surely ideological loyalties must have some importance, since a person's desires presumably govern the forecasts he makes? If this were the case, we would expect the opposition bloc (henceforth the center-liberal-conservative "bloc" is referred to as the opposition) in the Riksdag to predict a more rapid rate of internationalization than the social democrats. Table 6:2 shows that this is not the case. The politicians do in fact seem to represent a species of their own; they are more unlike the business executives, for example, than they are unlike one another.

On one point the results in Table 6:1 suggest a difference between politicians and trade union leaders. The latter predict a proportion of foreign business in Sweden considerably smaller than that expected by the former. This divergence can be explained to a great extent by the different ways in which the two camps view the foreign multinational companies. Roughly speaking, the politicians welcome the job opportunities and the technical

Table 6:2

	The situation today	In 10 years time according to the social democrats[2]	In 10 years time according to the opposition in the Riksdag[2]	In 10 years time according to the business executives[3]
Proportion of sales abroad for Swedish manufacturing companies (percent of total sales)	55[1]	64	62	69
Proportion of production abroad for Swedish manufacturing companies (percent of total production)	17[1]	24	24	31
Proportion of industrial employees in foreign-owned industry in Sweden (percent of total industrial employees)	10	15	17	—
Growth in Swedish manufacturing companies' production over the next 10 years (percent per year)	5.0[4]	4.5	5.1	8.0

[1] Unweighted mean value for the Swedish companies interviewed in 1972 ($n = 40$).
[2] Mean value for all respondents (18 social democrats, 8 opposition MPs).
[3] Unweighted mean value of evaluations by the business executives of their *own* company's future ($n = 40$).
[4] Mean value for the period 1960–1970.

know-how which the foreigners bring with them, while members of the wage-earner organizations fear the insensitivity of these companies to trade union action and suspect that such motives as a desire to acquire monopolies with a view to later closures may lie behind the operations of the multinationals. Many social democratic politicians commented on this disquiet in a rather paternalistic way. A typical response was: "I can understand that they're feeling a little uneasy just now, but it isn't really as bad as that, and anyway we can't do anything about it."

As we saw in the previous chapter, the forecasts of the top LO officials diverged from those of the lower ranks, in that the top officials predicted a more rapid rate for the internationalization of Swedish industry. We now find a similar situation in the social democratic party, where evaluations differ greatly between top officials in the government departments and members of parliament, with cabinet ministers occupying a position in between.

Table 6:3 shows that officials in the government bodies have much higher expectations about the rate of internationalization than the ordinary

Table 6:3

	The situation today	In 10 years time according to departmental officials (n = 6)	In 10 years time according to cabinet ministers (n = 5)	In 10 years time according to the members of parliament (n = 7)
Proportion of sales abroad for Swedish manufacturing companies (percent of total sales)	55[1]	69	63	59
Proportion of production abroad for Swedish manufacturing companies (per cent of total production)	17[1]	28	23	22
Proportion of industrial employees in foreign-owned industry in Sweden (percent of total industrial employment)	10	19	15	14
Growth in Swedish manufacturing companies' production over the next 10 years (percent per year)	5.3[3]	4.8	5.0	4.0

[1] Unweighted mean value for the Swedish companies interviewed in 1972 (n = 40).
[2] Mean value for all respondents.
[3] Mean value for the period 1960–1970.

members of parliament. In fact the estimates of these "experts" come very close to those of the business executives. One explanation of this may be that these departmental officials, particularly in the departments that interest us here, are the men who continually watch developments in industry, who come into contact with business executives and with international bodies—all of which can help to free them from the dramatic impact of the high figures. We will later discuss whether this divergence depends on differences in *value judgments* regarding the internationalization of business.

Legislation against the Multinational Corporations

One explanation of the relative modesty in the trade union leaders' forecasts of the rate of internationalization, in comparison with the forecasts of the business executives, was that these men expected a tightening-up of restrictions on the flow of investments over national borders. (*see* Chapter 5).

We can see from Table 6:4 that the same explanation applies to the politicians' forecasts.

A comparison with Table 5:3 (p. 92) shows that the estimates made by LO and the politicians agree closely, while the business executives believe

Table 6:4

"HOW WOULD YOU DESCRIBE SWEDISH POLICY TODAY, AND WHAT DO YOU THINK IT WILL BE LIKE IN TEN YEARS TIME IN THE FOLLOWING AREAS ... ?"

(Scale 1–5; 1 = very liberal; 5 = very restrictive)

	The situation today according to the politi- cians (n = 27)[1]	In 10 years time according to the politi- cians (n = 27)[1]	The situation today according to the business executives (n = 40)	In 10 years time according to the business executives (n = 40)
Trade policy	1.5	1.8	2.2	2.1
Policy towards the investments of Swedish companies in other countries	1.5	2.5	3.0	2.9
Policy towards foreign investments in Sweden	1.7	2.6	2.6	2.5
Policy towards the immigration and emigration of labor	2.0	2.7	2.8	2.9

[1] Mean values for all respondents.

in a considerably more liberal development. (However, it is important to note in this context that the business executives made their estimates during the winter of 1972-1973, i.e., before the oil crisis). The liberal and conservative parties predicted a little less restriction on investment policy, and the social democrats a little more, than the average shown in Table 6:4. The responses from the opposition reflect a mixture of beliefs and hope. Our respondents on that side of the Riksdag would like to see a more liberal policy but say that even if they came to power, they do not see how they could deviate in any radical way from the present course, which they see as a trend towards stricter regulation of international business. Even the conservative party, which is the most liberal-minded in these matters, admits that it would have to pursue a more "nationalistic" policy than it would really want to, so as not provoke its supporters. "Patriotism of the worst kind appears to some extent in all parties," says one representative of this party, and admits that some concessions to "the neo-chauvinistic trend" have to be made.

Many politicians expect to see not only measures provoked by the growth of the multinational corporations, but also a trend towards a more protectionistic trade policy in general. Other countries are only too readily blamed for this sort of development, but in fact there are politicians in all the four major parties who favor more protective measures to save threatened industries in Sweden in order to maintain a certain level of national self-sufficiency. There is no doubt that the oil crisis provided nourishment for this kind of neo-protectionism, and those who are probably most closely in touch with developments—namely the departmental officials—are also those who expect to see (again mainly in other countries) a halt in the liberalization of trade that has been taking place ever since the Second World War. The opposition parties regard this "state of emergency" type of thinking with mixed feelings. There is clearly a big difference here between centre party representatives and conservatives. The latter foresee with regret a move towards neo-protectionism and neo-mercantilism; but Centre Party members, together with the Social Democratic Parliamentary group, look upon a certain amount of restrictiveness on specific points as a fairly natural element in an otherwise relatively liberal world. This applies both to limited aspects of trade policy and to the issues that are being highlighted by the emergence of the large multinational corporations.

The Role of the Departmental Officials

It is tempting to try to explain the differences between the estimates of the future rate of internationalization put forward by the experts in the government departments and those put forward by Social Democratic members of the Riksdag in terms of their diverging views about future legislation—in the same way that we explained the differences between, for example, trade union people and business executives. Thus we would expect the officials who, as a group, predict a high rate of internationalization, to envisage a relatively liberal trade and investment policy. Our results show that this is not the case. Instead we find the opposite: the officials are the most "radical" in their forecasts about future legislation. This can be interpreted in two ways, both of which are supported by "soft data" from the interviews.

First, we could say that the people who have perceived the plans of the leading part for rapid foreign expansion are the same people who see the greatest need for regulating the companies concerned. For a small country like Sweden the socio-economic implications of internationalization will be so enormous that the representatives of all interests must take part in controlling developments: "We must have social controls;" "We must control developments without stopping them;" "We must protect ourselves in time." All these statements are typical of this attitude.

The second interpretation is that the under-secretaries and other experts in the public administration have assumed the role of intermediaries between industrial and economic interests on the one hand, and political and wage-earner interests on the other. Thus to satisfy all parties, they (since they are the people who design the control methods) must construct instruments which are formally restrictive but which can in fact be applied for quite liberal purposes. All but one of the members of a special group appointed to recommend new rules for the control of the multinational corporations have been interviewed as part of the present project, and we have received the definite impression that they do not regard their recommendation as especially restrictive, nor do they believe that it will greatly reduce the scope of Swedish foreign investments. The objections of the opposition parties and the business world have concerned this very point: that instruments are being designed which are not really necessary. Influential conservative politicians also feel that the recommendation has been made chiefly "for the sake of appearance, to satisfy calls for action from certain sections of the party," rather than as an expression of a desire to make any drastic changes in the situation of Swedish companies. This second inter- pretation of the role of the departmental officials agrees fairly closely with the way one trade union official described a previous foreign secretary's condemnation of investments in Portuguese colonies: he called it "an act put on for the people."

A further confirmation of this interpretation is the officials' positive attitude towards Scenario A, the laissez-faire world view. (We return below to the evaluations of the scenarios.)

THE SOCIAL DEMOCRATS' VIEW

Regardless of the motives behind the recommendation of the special committee mentioned above, it is clear that people in the Social Democratic party want to see stricter controls on the internationally operating companies. The principles on which they base their attitude accord with LO's view. They are not negative towards an international division of labour based on free trade and multinational production, but demand that the public interest should have some influence on decisions so that Swedish wage earners and Swedes in general should not suffer from the negative effects of the enormous structural changes that are said to accompany an unrestrained international industry. In the longer run, it is also claimed, the need to guard the interests of the democratic system and allow for the right of the developing countries to decide their own fates, calls for some restriction on the power of the private multinational corporations. The kind of control that is envisaged in the first instance is *to try each separate case on its own merits*, since it is not possible to make any general statements about the effects of Swedish foreign investments on employment and similar factors. In each case the main aspects to consider are employment and the structure of industry in Sweden. Aspects of foreign policy will not weigh particularly heavily; in this sphere it is so difficult to delimit the problems, and the effects of isolated Swedish actions are so small, that only such restrictions on investments as are sanctioned by the UN will be introduced in this context. It is interesting to find that once again there are big differences between the organizational levels in both the trade union movement and the Social Democratic party. The desire to introduce politically motivated restrictions on foreign investment, and the belief in the effectiveness of such measures, are considerably more marked at the local level in LO and among the grass roots in the social democratic Riksdag group.

The self-sufficiency argument has two centres of support. First, there is a group of politicians who see a genuine need to protect Sweden's "strategic" production. Secondly, there is a group which sees the self- sufficiency argument as a "loophole for considerations of employment" or as a chance to take some action contingent on the country's foreign policy when the international rules do not really permit it.

Another instrument of control which, it is believed, may eventually become relevant although never very widely used, consists of the state assuming part ownership in the multinational corporations (both Swedish parent companies and foreign subsidiaries in Sweden). Apparently, however, members of the Social Democratic party rely mainly on other control mechanisms rather than direct ownership. As far as the foreign companies are concerned, the demand will grow for more insight into company plans and actions, sometimes perhaps through state participation on the board of directors. In the case of the Swedish companies, it is expected that it will be possible to satisfy the need for insight and control by means of employee representation—and in certain cases state representation—on the board, combined with an extension of the system for granting permission for investment projects abroad in the Foreign Exchange Control Board. (Employees are already represented by two members on the board of directors in Swedish companies with more than 25 employees.)

Although state ownership is not seen either as a goal in itself or as an effective or suitable means of controlling the multinational corporations, a considerable increase in state participation in industrial operations is nevertheless predicted. The main reason for this is the enormous need for capital for future investments; another related reason is the rising cost of research and development work. The need to maintain industrial employment will also lead to an increase in state participation in industrial operations, partly by means of new investments and partly by the "rescue" of companies threatened with closure, possibly by pumping in financial support from the pension funds we have referred to previously. One member of the government expressed a fear that the pension funds might be used in this defensive way rather than to ensure social control over the multinational corporations for example: "The trade unions, who will decide how these funds should be used, only think about local employment, so the money will not be used in any really far-sighted way."

Another argument for an expanding state-owned industrial sector is that trade and collaboration will be increasing with the developing countries and many Eastern countries, and it is best to handle business with countries of this kind at government level. This, at least, is the opinion of many influential Social Democrats. Sweden is said to have advantages over other countries in this respect, because of its political neutrality and because the developing countries regard Sweden as setting an example in many ways among the industrial nations. Furthermore, Sweden is competent in the building and selling of large systems of products and services, e.g., turnkey plants, which will be very much in demand particularly in the Eastern countries. This turn towards new markets is felt to be both economically advantageous ("We have the technology and they have the raw materials—we complement one another.") and politically desirable.

As for comparative advantages in other respects, there is a general tendency among leading Social Democrats to regard these as dependent on political decisions. For example, Sweden's tough environmental legislation may lead to business opportunities for Swedish companies which will have learned in good time to make products that other countries will ultimately also need. Another factor in the competitive situation is Sweden's peaceful labor market. Conservative politicians have much less faith in this socio-political product-cycle theory. They define Sweden's comparative advantages instead in "harder" terms, such as access to a well-educated workforce, advanced technology and a good education system.

Moreover, there is a tendency among the conservatives to predict a rapid deterioration in Sweden's competitive stance. High marginal tax rates, which make it difficult to maintain research and development activities (because they frighten away foreign experts who do not wish to live here, and encourage Swedes to move abroad) were mentioned by many politicians in the opposition.

Anxiety about the multinational corporations is, as we have already seen, more widespread and stronger in LO than in the Social Democratic party. With the exception of a few top officials and members of the government, politicians see no immediate or dangerous threat to the Swedish economy or the Swedish political system in the activities of the multinational companies. Even those who are most critical of the multinationals consider that the problem is trivial in Sweden and in all industrialized countries compared with the implications of international business on economic, political and social developments in the developing countries. One Social Democrat put it bluntly: "The MNCs should not be permitted to operate in the developing countries; they live on the enormous profits they make there." The predominant attitude is that Sweden must *guard itself against possible future dangers*. Internationalism is acknowledged as a principle, but there must be measures of control to ensure that internationalization does not take place solely on the companies' terms.

In the same way as LO, the Social Democrats prefer international frame-works for control activities but they are extremely pessimistic about the prospects of being able to design a control system with effective sanctions on the international level within the foreseeable future. Therefore, this task must be carried out in the first place on the national level, but "national interests are not the same as nationalism." On the contrary, Sweden is regarded as a very internationally-minded country. Just like the business executives, the Social Democratic politicians identify the USA and France as the great potential protectionists and nationalists in the world. The ethnocentric Scenario B is rejected as both improbable and very unfor-tunate—in fact, it is rejected more firmly by the Social Democrats than by the opposition. The Social Democrats also consistently regard Scenario B as a possible expression of conservative political forces in Sweden, particularly in the Centre Party.

The reaction to Scenario C, the regulatory scenario, further underlines the picture of an internationally-minded Social Democratic party. The desirability ratings reveal that something similar to the international Scenario C is a goal, and the assessment of effects on foreign sales and foreign produc-tion show that the scenario is not thought to describe a world negative to all international business.

The assessments of the effects of the liberal Scenario A on the Swedish economy confirm that opinions about the legislation against international business the next ten years are likely to witness do lead the Social Democrats and the business executives to rather different visions of the scope of this kind of activity. In Scenario A, the social democrats' forecasts are adjusted upward and approach those of the business executives which gives us reason to assume that it is not—or at least it is not only—the method of investigation that produces the differences. (see Table 6:7).

THE OPPOSITION'S VIEW

As was to be expected, the opposition parties viewed the problems that accompany the internationalization of industry much less seriously than did the Social Democrats. Anxiety on this question appears to decline as we move from left to right along the whole political spectrum. At the same time there are a number of differences within the opposition bloc which will have important implications for us later, when we come to analyze the way in which the total set of expectations and plans determines the dynamic characteristics that define Sweden's stance vis-à-vis the future.

If we may judge from our admittedly incomplete data, it seems that the Centre Party embraces certain attitudes which differ in kind from those held in all the other parties. Social democracy and communism have their roots in international socialism; liberalism, with its faith in the mobility of production factors inside and over national boundaries, has its faithful adherents in the liberal party and among the conservatives; but the Centre Party has no similar ideological base. We could almost say that because of the party's emphasis on local interests, there is a certain degree of ethnocentrism in its very being. Furthermore, and this is important in an area where developments occur very quickly, most of the party's officials are new; no traditions have had time to form, and so far no experts on such complicated questions as the problems of internationalization have emerged. Nor can the party's traditional supporters, the farmers, be said to represent any notable element in the free trade tradition.

Furthermore, there is no doubt that the party does operate partly as a refuge for voters who are dissatisfied, in particular with the social democratic policy. The absence of an established ideology, combined with the popularity that national and nationalistic measures can achieve among the party's potential voters, make the Centre Party the only party in Swedish politics which can be expected to follow a genuinely nationalistic and protectionistic path. The party is a sort of natural haven for a motley set of dissatisfied groups—the opponents of bureaucracy and the big-city mentality as well as people more fundamentally opposed to the kind of civilization represented by the industrial world.

Our interviews, and other studies, support the hypothesis that opposition to a protectionist and ethnocentric policy is not a notable charateristic of the Centre Party. There does not seem to be any really fundamental view on these matters; instead, the party would prefer to rely on some kind of pragmatic day-to-day policy, into which the proposals of the special committee mentioned above would in fact fit rather well. Moreover, because of the party's local image, a Centre-dominated government would possibly apply the instruments designed by the Social Democrats more strictly and more conscientiously than the designers might have expected.

The liberal party regards the multinational threat not as a function of supranational activities in themselves, but as a consequence of a tendency towards monopolistic or oligopolistic market forms on a global level.[3] Thus the solution is not to stop companies from operating internationally, but to work for stricter legislation against any restriction on competition, both internationally and in Sweden. With such a policy, no *special* rules concerning, for example, the foreign companies in Sweden would be needed. Thus the Liberal Party has not taken a classical laissez-faire attitude towards these questions. Scenario A, for example, is regarded as far from perfect — a world in which major conflicts arise and giant corporations have far too much power. Scenario C is actually seen as more or less as good, despite objections in the Liberal Party towards the "corporativist" element, i.e., the absence of influence exercised by individual people.

Typical of the Liberal Party's attitude, as well as of the conservatives', is the tendency to blame possible problems in Sweden due to the international activities of the companies on a wrong-headed anti-business economic policy on the part of the government. The effect of the marginal tax rates on the location of research and development has already been mentioned, and other examples were also given by our respondents. But perhaps the most important, they felt, was that the general climate of opinion in Sweden was so unfavorable to the corporations. (It should perhaps be mentioned here that people in the social democratic camp accuse the conservatives of putting the idea that they are living in a hostile environment into the heads of the business leaders. For example, in the case of trade with eastern countries and developing countries, one minister called for more activity on the part of the companies in establishing collaboration with the government.)

The Liberal Party must be regarded as an internationalist force in Swedish politics. Nevertheless, given the internal difficulties in the party and the reliance placed on liberal economic and political principles, a downswing in business activity, with its threat of unemployment and a simultaneous increase in the foreign activities of Swedish industry, might make it difficult for the party to compete with the down-to-earth message of its ally, the centre party.

The ambivalent attitude of the liberal party to the laissez-faire scenario is evidence of the fact that the great changes taking place in the global economic system will have such enormous consequences on political and social conditions on our planet, that established political doctrines will be of limited value in assessing and evaluating developments. Given the objectives of the liberal party, the purely liberal doctrine does not altogether fit in a world where such strong forces have been set in motion that exclusive reliance on market forces as the means of control could result in major structural disturbances. (If we interpret the liberal doctrine as Adam Smith once did, assuming that it encompasses very active efforts on the part of the state to ensure competition, then the argument is of course different.)

The Conservatives show the most understanding attitude towards the multinational corporations. They (the Conservatives) like to regard themselves as the only true liberal party in Swedish politics, and they are only too ready to blame the opposition bloc for deviations from liberal principles. We have previously mentioned that the Conservatives regard inadequately informed voters who are receptive to nationalistic rhetoric as a restriction on their actions. However, there is also in the party, particularly perhaps in the lower ranks, a genuine "Swedishness," an admiration for Swedish traditions and a loyalty to the "mother country" that are somewhat reminiscent of the "green wave" trends that have given the Centre Party so many new voters. For these two reasons we cannot expect that even the conservatives will always defend unlimited freedom of movement for international business.

In a predominant place in the thinking of the Conservative Party, and indeed in the Liberal Party, we find the belief that it is dangerous for Sweden to pursue a policy deviating from that of other Western countries. If Sweden introduces restrictions that strike at companies in other countries (restrictions on foreign takeovers of Swedish-owned corporations, for example) or at the economies of other countries (by regulating the foreign investments of Swedish companies for example), then the country would have to expect to be subjected to retaliatory measures of a similar kind. An unpleasant process reminiscent of the trade wars of the 1930's would be launched, always assuming that Sweden was not completely isolated. The Social Democrats have much more faith in Sweden's ability to act independently. For one thing, they do not see the problem as a zero-sum game in which one nation's gain must inevitably be another's loss. In other words, they consider that *all* countries should be able to benefit from placing international business under the watchful and controlling eye of society. According to this view, the question of who is actually exporting jobs, for example, is of minor importance. The important point instead is to design a system of control over the structural changes that accompany internationalization in *all* countries. Obviously, according to this view, developments in Sweden are not so different from developments in other countries, and these other countries can, therefore, be expected to understand any restrictions and controls Sweden might have to impose.

Sweden is regarded in both the political blocs as a relatively liberal country. There is a particularly clear tendency to see Sweden as a country which is "honest" on international matters. Sweden's legislation which is formally strict but liberal in application, is often contrasted with the rules of some other countries which are formally liberal but in practice governed by hard national egotism. Conservative politicians see the arguments of the special committee on multinational corporations as a deviation from the earlier line and a break with Sweden's international obligations, for instance in OECD; the Social Democrats on the other hand see them as providing greater room for manoeuvres within the frameworks of standing agreements. Typical remarks from influential Social Democrats are: "OECD's capital-liberalization code went a little too far during the 1960s;" "We are now doing what all the other countries were doing all the time;" "The liberalism of the 1950s and 1960s was simply naïvete." Furthermore the Social Democrats, and particularly leading members of the party, point out the opportunities for companies to redirect their operations towards new markets if conditions on the traditional markets are disturbed. The developing countries and the eastern nations represent markets unaffected by the internal controversies of the Western world, and where buyers prefer to discuss with state employees rather than with private capitalists. Moreover, the leading Social Democrats regard the free-trade agreement concluded with EEC as a guarantee that there will be no really serious disturbances on these most important hunting-grounds for Swedish industry. Quite clearly, political evaluations of a reorientation to the south and east provide part of the explanation, together with the diverging interpretations of the multinational problematique that we referred to above, of the differences in attitude in the various political parties towards unilateral Swedish action.

Apart from the risk of countermeasures from other countries, concern for the competitiveness of Swedish industry is one reason why the opposition parties, particularly the Conservative Party, have rejected the ideas presented by the special committee. It is felt that the bureaucratic machinery required to test each separate application for foreign investment would only make things even more difficult for business companies, hard pressed as they already are by foreign competition. Speed and secrecy in decision-making would be lost, even if the decisions themselves might well be good ones in the end. Furthermore, it is feared by members of the Liberal and Conservative parties felt that the testing of applications might come to be used as a political weapon or, worse still, as a forum where wage-earner representatives and politicians from a variety of parties could flaunt short-sighted partial interests, waving the national flag and citing the "good of the country" (or the region) as a sales argument.

The Communist Party is regarded by many conservatives and some social Democratic politicians as the only force in Sweden working for an ethnocentric protectionistic world. However, to judge from statements made at our interview with this party's representative, it appears that on the contrary the Communist Party is an internationally-minded party. Its attitude is that free trade and an international division of labor do not necessarily presuppose a positive view of the multinational corporations. Since we only interviewed one communist member of the Riksdag, we cannot base any definite conclusions on our material alone. However, a study of the party's history, its programmes and its behavior in parliament shows that the accusations of protectionism and nationalism that were often directed at the communist party during our interviews with the business executives, the trade union leaders and, in particular, with the conservative politicians, have very little basis in historical reality—at least if we look at the party's attitude as a whole. On the other hand, there are many situations in which the distinction made by the communist party between protectionism and control of monopolistic-capitalistic companies is of no practical significance. For example, the party often has to decide in the Riksdag between two propositions, both of them bad from their own point of view. It is then easy to imagine that rather than tolerate a proposal favoring the freedom of movement of private capital while promoting free-trade, the party prefers to accept a proposal containing both protectionistic and company-restrictive elements. This situation is

Table 6:5

PROBABILITY FOR SCENARIOS A, B AND C

(Scale 1–5; 1 = not at all probable; 5 = very probable)

	Scenario A	Scenario B	Scenario C
Social democrats[1, 2] ($n = 18$)	2.7	1.7	2.7
Opposition politicians[2] ($n = 8$)	2.6	2.1	2.9
LO[2] ($n = 25$)	2.7	2.2	2.9

[1] Includes also departmental officials.
[2] Mean value for all respondents.

rather reminiscent of the attitude of the shop stewards to Scenario B, which they regarded as a poor alternative that would have to be accepted for lack of a better one.

THE POLITICIANS ON THE SCENARIOS—PROBABILITY AND DESIRABILITY

The arguments above were based on results from the interview material as a whole, but it could also be interesting to look in particular at the views of the politicians on the scenarios. In Table 6:5 the probability ratings for some groups have been summarized.

The remarkable thing about the results in Table 6:5 is the agreement between the groups. Scenario A and Scenario C are regarded as roughly equal as regards probability, while Scenario B is thought to be somewhat less probable. Scenario C clearly stands out as something of a synthesis of the expectations in all groups in Swedish society. (As we shall see in more detail in Chapter 7, there is also a tendency among the business executives to see Scenario C as an acceptable and probable compromise.) However, although people more or less agree about the shape the future will ultimately assume, they by no means agree about how it *ought* to be (*see* Table 6:6).

We can see from Table 6:6 that Scenario A and Scenario C change places in the desirability rankings of the Social Democrats and the opposition parties. In view of the size of the material, the differences that the figures suggest within the various groups are not very reliable. However, they are supported by other results and analyses, so it is at least possible to take them as a basis for building hypotheses. The clearest of these differences lies between groups inside the social democratic party. The experts who will be chiefly responsible for designing policy vis-à-vis the multinational corporations are relatively positive in their attitude towards the liberal Scenario A. At the same time they are also the people who foresee most restrictions in this area. This may perhaps support the interpretation that we suggested above of the role played by these officials, namely that they act as intermediaries between different opinions, as administrators

Table 6:6

DESIRABILITY OF SCENARIOS A, B AND C

(Scale 1–5: 1 = not at all desirable; 5 = very desirable)

	Scenario A	Scenario B	Scenario C
Social democrats[1] ($n = 18$)	3.1	1.3	4.3
... of which officials ($n = 6$)	3.8	1.4	4.0
cabinet minister ($n = 5$)	3.0	1.5	4.0
members of the Riksdag ($n = 7$)	2.7	1.2	4.8
Opposition politicians[1] ($n = 8$)	4.0	1.6	3.1
... of which centre party members[2]			
($n = 2$)	4.0	2.5	3.5
liberal party members[2] ($n = 3$)	3.3	1.0	3.3
conservatives[2] ($n = 3$)	5.0	1.5	2.5

[1] Mean value for all respondents.
[2] The values for the individual opposition parties are very uncertain and can only be regarded as an indication on which to base hypotheses, and as an illustration of the qualitative results presented above.

of compromise, and as designers of political tools to satisfy all camps. This may suggest a rather unkind picture of a group of professional tightrope walkers; in fact, what we find in the top ranks of the public administration are a few people who combine a conservative or liberal political view with loyalty to the government and a wish to fulfill its political intentions. The pattern in remarkably similar to the one that we found in the trade union movement, where the leading functionaries were much more positive towards Scenario A than the "lower" levels were. Thus in general there appears to be a gap between the ruling and the voting camps in the various organizations when it comes to their evaluations of a clearly liberal economic future.

Worth noting among the dissimilarities within the opposition bloc is the Liberal Party's ambivalent attitude to the global liberal Scenario A, and the Centre Party's rather watered-down rejection of the protectionistic Scenario B. What attracted the Centre Party in this scenario was the peaceful, static state it described and the possibilities it was thought to provide for maintaining national and regional identities. Without wanting to read too much into the results, we would like to put forward the hypothesis that the Centre Party is the only party in Swedish politics not clearly opposed on principle to protectionistic measures. A rather similar attitude can also be found among certain elements in the Social Democratic party, but the leading groups in this party are much more internationally-minded than the equivalent groups in the centre party.

THE EFFECT OF THE SCENARIOS
ON SWEDISH INDUSTRY

The forecasts linked to alternative scenarios provide an interesting illustration of how interpretations of world views can differ. First, we can see

Table 6:7

	The situation today	In 10 years time	Scenario A	Scenario B	Scenario C
Proportion of sales abroad for Swedish manufacturing companies (percent of total sales)					
Social democrats (n = 18)	55[1]	64	64	50	63
Opposition politicians (n = 8)	55	62	65	49	58
Proportion of production abroad for Swedish manufacturing companies (percent of total production)					
Social democrats (n = 18)	17[1]	24	25	17	23
Opposition politicians (n = 8)	17	24	26	15	21
Proportion employed in foreign-owned industry in Sweden (percent of total industrial employment)					
Social democrats (n = 18)	10	15	16	10	14
Opposition politicians (n = 8)	10	17	18	9	12
Growth in Swedish manufacturing companies' production over the next ten years (percent per year)					
Social democrats (n = 18)	5.0[3]	4.5	4.4	3.1	4.8
Opposition politicians (n = 8)	5.0	5.1	5.5	3.0	4.7

[1] Unweighted mean value for the Swedish companies interviewed in 1972 (n = 40).
[2] Mean value for all respondents.
[3] Rough average for the period 1960–1970.

from Table 6:7 that both political camps see Scenario A as speeding up the process of industrial internationalization. Secondly, the opposition parties see in Scenario C a restrictive world, while the Social Democrats see more of a controlled internationalistic world. This difference may indicate that the social democratic party has supplied inadequate information about the future that it really wants. Another explanation could be that both parties, more or less consciously, have tried to envisage "suitable" consequences for the particular scenario that they would prefer to see realized. It should also be mentioned that the opposition's view of the consequences of Scenario C are shared to some extent by the under-secretaries—an agreement which was to be expected in light of our earlier discussion.

By far the most important result in Table 6:7, however, is the over-whelming agreement about the effects of a protectionistic world. To begin with, all parties and groups predict a very much lower rate of growth in Scenario B than in any of the other worlds. Secondly, the politicians in the protectionistic scenario, almost without exception, considerably scale down their forecasts of the proportion of production abroad. Thus on this point Scenario B is regarded as an effective policy. The usual motivation for a development such as that depicted in Scenario B is probably to stop employment being "exported" to other countries and, in view of the consequences that the politicians say they would expect this to have, the alternative that "closes the frontiers" is not as irrational as it appears if we judge it in terms of the business executives' world views and in terms of their theories about companies' behavior. The view of the politicians agrees very closely with that of the trade union leaders. (see p. 98). There are also some intra-group differences. It seems that certain under-secretaries and ministers, together with conservative politicians, have more faith in the immunity of companies to national restrictions than the other politicians have.

SUMMARY

To summarize, the results of the study support the assumption that in relation to the multinational corporations the political system is a lagging system, in the sense that its forecasts of future developments in international industrial activity are considerably more modest than the statements of the business executives would lead us to expect. (Obviously, however, this is not a sufficient reason for defining a system as lagging.) Furthermore, Swedish members of parliament are both less knowledgeable and less worried than members of the Swedish trade union movement about the phenomenon of the multinational corporations. Nevertheless there is a heterogeneity in the political system, related to differences in rank and degree of expertise rather than to differences in party loyalties. If we disregard the Communist Party, the gap between the established parliamentary parties is not particularly wide at the present time. As the internationalization of the leading system speeds up, however, we may expect that potential elements of conflict—which have at present barely been perceived even by the politicians themselves—will emerge more clearly. Leading elements in the Social Democratic camp, and in the Liberal and Conservative parties, have given clear indications of their aspirations and objectives in connection with the future of the global industrial system. Apart from a few special points mentioned above, Scenario C and Scenario A respectively provide fairly good approximations of attitudes in the two camps. In the Centre Party, on the other hand, there is no correspondingly clear vision based on ideology and traditions. Because this party lacks theories and expertise and nurses an ambition to decentralize decision-making to local levels, Scenario B represents the closest approximation to its policy in dynamic terms, although the state depicted in this scenario is certainly not regarded as any kind of ideal. That Scenario B is an alternative which cannot be immediately ignored, although many parties oppose it on principle, is confirmed by the belief that almost all the politicians concur in the inhibiting effect of the protectionistic world on multinational business. This also provides some support for our theoretical argument in Chapter 2, where we suggested that business is the leading part and that the administrators of the nation states and the wage-earner movements are all sitting in the same boat.

NOTES

1. The "Saltsjöbaden Agreement" of 1938 provided the basis for the era of peaceful industrial relations that has characterized the Swedish labor market for a long time. The agreement regulated the negotiation system and codified the principle of collective bargaining. It also signalled the coming of an atmosphere of cooperation and general mutual understanding between the parties of the labor market.
2. See Veckans Affärer, 16–19, 1973, where the most important results of the survey were reported.
3. The reader should be careful not to interpret "liberal" to mean what this term usually means in the USA. In Europe, Liberals and Conservatives are often allies in government or opposition against Social Democrats or Socialists, or they take up a position in between the socialist and the conservative blocs. The liberal party of Sweden is comparable—as far as its relative position on the "left-right scale" is concerned—to the FDP in West Germany and the Liberal Party in Great Britain.

7

Dissonances in the Internationalization Problematique: A Synthesis of Future Views

A REFERENCE PROJECTION

The results reported in Chapters 4–6 are interesting in themselves as reflections of expectations, evaluations and plans regarding the future in powerful groups in Swedish society. However, given our view that the creation of futures is a process in which subsystems in the global system interact with one another, and our belief that there are complex relationships between plans and expectations in the various parts of the total system, it becomes necessary also to examine the results of the three phases in an overall perspective. To understand the future one must understand the present; at the same time, however, it is the future consequences of present circumstances that determine the character of the present (or, at least, those attributes of the present which are interesting from the planning point of view).

To be able to define the internationalization problematique we, therefore, have to understand how present ideas about internationalization will affect the future. The technique we have used to analyse the way in which current attitudes and behavior in various parts of society interact and shape future developments, is called *reference projection*.

By a reference projection we mean a projection of present conditions on to the future, i.e., a description of the next ten years based on the assumption that there will be *no fundamental changes in attitudes, values, plans and behavior patterns* in the subsystems of Swedish society that we have analysed here. The aim of the reference projection is not to provide a forecast but, by projecting the present on to the screen of the future, to *define the problems* surrounding the emerging global industrial system. The reference projection is a tool which, by revealing dissonances and consonances, can help us to determine the character of the present. These properties of the present are determined and identified by the shape they assume in the future. The method can therefore be said to reverse the usual causal relationship between the tenses. The future determines the present, instead of being determined by the present. From our normative point of departure this is a convenient approach, since it is still possible to shape the future but not the present.

The reference projection is only a starting point for a further analysis, for a critique aimed at identifying *alternatives* to the reference scenario. Given our unrealistic assumption of stability, it is probable that the result of a reference projection—in a time and in an area characterized by rapid change—will in many important respects imply an undesirable view of the future. After all, the method involves "blowing up" the problems of the present so that we can identify them more easily and perhaps be able to counteract them before it is too late. Thus, the "forecast" which is made in a reference projection is *self-obstructing.* Our critical inspection of the reference scenario, and the alternative futures the critique generates, together suggest programmes for action in the global industrial system. We try to discover and invent factors which resolve the dissonances revealed by the reference projection and which together lead towards a state that can be regarded as desirable—or at any rate tolerable—by the majority of the decision-makers whose actions determine future developments. We have also made it a condition that the recommendations arising out of our dissonance-reducing factors (and which we will later present in concrete form addressed to the relevant key groups) should appear feasible to put into effect during the next ten years.

Since the interview results which provide the basis for the reference projection are predominantly qualitative, the analysis of the interaction between the groups will also be qualitative. This makes it difficult for the reader to check how much "objective data" really does underpin the reference projection, since we are prevented for reasons of space and confidentiality from reporting all the unprocessed data (*see* Chapter 3, for a discussion of reliability and validity in futures studies). Not even an intuitively perceived agreement between the subresults in Chapters 4–6 and the analysis in the reference projection provides a complete guarantee of a "correct" manipulation of data, since the most critical step in a study of such a complex phenomenon as the future internationalization of business is probably the researcher's identification of *relevant* data, and this selection can, of course, be made in different ways by different people. However, the reader can examine the theories on which our data collection was based, although it is still probably not possible to claim that the analysis is incontrovertible even within the bounds of a book such as this. To reinforce our argument we have therefore described in detail our reasons for making just this reference projection and no other (pp. 128–131).

To underline the connection with the results of our interviews, we have transformed the rather abstract material into a more concrete and digestible form before going on to the theoretical analysis. To present the contents of the reference projection we will let a fictitious character—the experienced journalist, M. Polsnok, domestic reporter at a well-known Swedish newspaper—talk to our readers in his own column in the Sunday edition of 17th of October, 1984. The reference projection describes a train of events in Sweden. The picture of the situation abroad is based on the same assumptions we have already mentioned, namely that there has been no fundamental change in the policies, attitudes, etc., of the actors in the global industrial system. To some extent this analysis is based on the results of our sister studies in the USA and Finland. (It should be noted that the *environment* of the total system is supposed to be dynamic. In other words, in the reference projection we expect that technological development, business cycles, etc., will occur as usual.)

We would like to stress that any possible resemblance between the characters in the reference projection and any persons now living or dead is purely coincidental. The attributes of the actors are determined by certain general attributes of the type of organizations they represent.

Dear Reader,

Most of you have certainly long since forgotten—or perhaps have never even asked yourselves—how we got into this situation. Don't be upset by your thoughtlessness! There are reasons for it, many of them completely beyond your control. Most of those who were involved have, for obvious reasons, kept quiet about their part in it, and our excellent press naturally does not wish to spread national discord by turning our Swedish society's legally and democratically elected representatives inside out. So hold on, for your very own M. Polsnok is now going to tell you a story from the annals of Swedish history.

It all began so well; 1974 was a good year with high export incomes for Swedish industry, employment rising to heights that no one had dreamt of in the first uncertain months of the year. The Minister of Finance was beaming, sometimes making generous gifts, and sometimes gently putting the brakes on the gaily twirling wheels of our Swedish economy. The proposition for tighter control on applications for permission to invest abroad was accepted by the Riksdag without any great controversy, thanks to the agreement reached between the governing party and the largest party in the opposition. Nobody dreamt then what the consequences of this agreement would be! Because of the splendid rise in employment and the favorable export figures, the Foreign Exchange Control Board never saw any reason to interfere in the foreign investments, and in any case most of the members silently felt it was hopeless to make a "correct" judgement in any particular case. And in many people's eyes this was not the job of the Control Board anyway. Social control and wage-earner influence were the slogans, and it was all right to take socio-economic aspects into account, as long as the national economy was functioning well, as it was. Admittedly there were loudmouths in LO and young whipper-snappers among the Social Democrats who complained of the "laxity" that the board showed during the first year. And admittedly there were odd people hanging around the outskirts of the Centre Party who spoke of "all-round economic structure," "local community" or even "self-sufficiency." These people were firmly ticked off by the opinion-leaders and found it difficult to make themselves heard in debates, but somehow they managed to achieve great popularity. Nobody in the party dared enter upon a polemic with the acknowledged opinion-leaders, so an embarassed silence quickly spread over the debate. Alas, how wise the centre's "decision" to reserve these sentiments for coming times appears today!

Then came 1976, with business activity on the decline, rising unemployment which again was beginning to be referred to as "structural," and an uneasy foreign-policy situation. The USA was having difficulty with its balance of trade, the Japanese were meeting increasingly strong opposition in Southeast Asia and Latin America, and EEC's "clock" threatened not only to stop but even to go into reverse. Swedish companies had used the business boom to acquire room for manoeuvres by starting subsidiaries, however small, in most of the major countries. Production in the foreign subsidiaries had increased dramatically, without anyone really noticing. The large foreign multinational corporations had also been able to expand undisturbed in Sweden, chiefly by buying up Swedish companies. In the general rejoicing that broke out when the domesday prophets of the "oil crisis" (in 1973–74 the oilproducing countries and the oil companies sharply increased the price of crude oil, which was regarded by the people of the time as a crisis) turned to other activities and the happy optimism of the 1960s appeared to be returning, all the reservations which had been directed against "internationalization" by trade union people and social democrats were forgotten.

It was really a question of who would think of it first. The youth organization of the Social Democratic party had mentioned the matter to the Prime Minister at the end of 1975, but in the eyes of the public it was the leader of the Centre Party who really launched the idea. "If we have exported trucks from Sweden before, we can go on doing it" he said, thereby stopping plans for the billion-kroner investments in the USA. LO kept quiet, despite violent attacks from the American automobile workers' union. Shortly afterwards the USA raised the duties on the import of trucks by 50 percent which, when things began to get sticky in the Swedish automobile industry, seemed to give further support to the centre's argument that: "We must anyway keep some manufacturing in the country, and with the troubled situation today we must think about the future and safeguard ourselves against possible blockade." The Social Democrats could not simply sit silently, watching the Centre Party carry off all the laurels by their skillful exploitation of the Social Democrats' own 1974 laws (about the testing of every application for investment by the Currency Exchange Board).

At last, during the election campaign, they conveniently found a case which they could turn down—thus proving their own energy and vigour. After that the round-abouts began to spin again. The Centre Party put their chief ideologists on the job and they managed to make the party's attitude sound as if it had some sort of consistency. "More self-control and more self-sufficiency." "Sweden must remain an independent country." "The developing countries need their own food—grow more sugar-beet in Sweden." All these slogans swept across Sweden in a wave of enthusiasm.

LO was taken unaware. Admittedly the metal workers' trade union had made a fuss in November 1975, but in general the top men in LO had watched developments quite calmly. To the trade union leaders' horror, the Centre Party now won several local union elections. Although this only happened in a few companies—which for some obscure reason felt themselves threatened by closures because of planned expansion abroad—the results were grist to the mill of the radicals in the trade union movement. The liberal LO economists were now really feeling the pinch and they spent a lot of time writing after-dinner speeches and attending congresses. "The LO bosses must show a bit more spirit" was the cry—and so they did. The old-fashioned, simple and honourable men who had long remained in the shadow of the clever speakers and the brilliant and subtle politicians now got their chance to seize important positions in LO, with the support of the radical forces they had so often scorned in their speeches. Talk of safeguarding national employment, the national economy and—ultimately—the nation itself, sounded better in the mouths of these strong men and of the members of the Centre Party than in those of the Social Democratic leaders who were generally regarded as technocrats or bureaucrats. For this reason the election campaign began very gloomily for the government party.

Moreover, many Social Democrats doubted the wisdom of pressing the companies so hard and so arbitrarily, as the parties vied with one another for the title of "Sweden's Most Swedish Party" which was developing in the Currency Exchange Board. When EEC suddenly demanded action against Sweden's discriminatory policy, many ministers and high departmental officials really did begin to move warily. On the other hand, for the young radicals this was the final proof that the free trade agreement was simply another example of the European Community's octopus tactics. And then, just before the statutory industrial holiday, a large German manufacturer of electrical equipment closed down its operations in Sweden—on the grounds, it was said, that Sweden had raised the duties on certain articles (which it had done, as a fair answer to similar measures on the part of the USA). After that, word went out from the Social Democratic campaign headquarters that the fight against multinational capitalism was to be a key issue in the election. Great enthusiasm broke out among the younger election workers. At last, a chance to fight! There was some embarassment in the Centre Party, which now found itself arguing for the same cause as the Social Democrats, but on quite different grounds. The government party's marginal groups, however, were frightened into the Centre fold by a series of leftist forays, mostly on the part of the more youthful enthusiasts. In common with the Centre Party, the voters preferred to blame high unemployment on the poor administration of the country and on those dreadful foreigners, rather than—in common with the Social Democrats and the Communists—on capitalism.

As we all know, the Centre Party won the election in the autumn of 1976. The world outside our country was much the same as it is today, eight years later. Countries and blocs quarrelled sometimes about one thing, sometimes about another; trading policy became a major means of exerting pressure and was applied on an eye-for-an-eye and a tooth-for-a-tooth basis. In the industrialized world economic growth was very modest; in the developing countries it was more or less nil. In the international organs there was such a deadlock that even cocktail parties called for extremes of political caution. In many countries populist movements were having great success.

Many Swedish politicians began to regret the exaggerated nationalistic promises that they had let themselves in for during the election campaign. Only the ideologists of the government party were optimistic, and their voices could be heard more and more often in the various cultural and social debates. The active debaters of the old days, on the other hand, were getting tired. What could they do now in the new political climate?

Suddenly, there came a shock: a report on the effects of the wave of restrictiveness during 1976. Towards the autumn of 1977 the Prime Minister received a document in which it was writ clear and large that production in the foreign subsidiaries of Swedish companies had increased *more rapidly* during the last year than during any previous year! And what was more, despite the efforts of the Currency Exchange Control Board to maintain Swedish employment, exports had dropped dramatically! It had been easy for the big multinational corporations to get round the restrictions; the truck-manu-facturing plant had been built in collaboration with a German company. Only the small companies had suffered in any way from the protectionistic tendencies in Sweden and other countries—and this so much so that their very existence was threatened.

You can easily imagine, dear reader, how difficult it was for the Centre Party leader to explain this to the electorate. The new government must be able to show an improvement in the employment figures soon, but how was it to be done? Even the foreign companies were deserting Sweden, because although it was difficult for the competitors to force our barriers to trade, our market was too small to motivate any major investment.

Businessmen had complained bitterly about the uninformed debate on "inter-nationalization," and no one could mistake the satisfaction with which they viewed the confusion spreading among politicians on the publication of *The Effect of Econo-mic-Political Measures on the Multinational Corporations—A Study of Swedish Policy during 1976*. Liberals and Conservatives who had kept quiet during the election campaign, in order to enjoy the sweets of power, suddenly cried: "What did we tell you?" And the left of the Social Democratic party cried: "Business has failed Sweden— socialize the multinationals!"

After many attempts to reach a compromise between incompatible political opinions in the four major parties, the social democrats returned comfortably to power in 1979. They pursued by and large the same policy as the centre party. Certainly some members of the new government must have felt: "For God's sake let us have an end to this neo-protectionism." But Sweden was by now enmeshed in controversies with practically every other country—and they in turn involved in controversies with one another—so that it was extremely difficult to find a way out of the mess. Apart from this, the radicals in the party had their own ideas about how the corporations should be made to show their "loyalty to society," and in the radical package there was no room for liberal policies. And there was still the problem of guarding against Centre Party success in the trade union movement, where the party's emphasis on local and regional interests was popular. This made it impossible to deviate from the restrictive treatment of foreign investment administered by the Currency Exchange Control Board.

And this, my friends, is how things have gone on ever since. The only winners have been the multinational corporations. (You all remember, of course, how the big computer company was lured here on very favourable terms by the Minister of Industry, and how this assured the Social Democratic victory in 1982 by creating five thousand new job opportunities at one blow?) Governments all over the world are busy trying to remain in power and pecking away at each other; and trade union bosses all have so much trouble with their local branches that they have to stick to very short-sighted policies. The ICFTU is no more than a forum for pretty speeches on festive occasions. The United Nations is split into two camps: the rich against the poor. In brief, the only international force in the world today is the multinational corporations, whose profits this year have achieved fantastic heights. (For this information we can thank a poor economist working at the University of Heidelberg. He has patiently checked up on all the mock purchases and mock sales, the mergers, closures and changes of name, etc., which have taken place in the international business world in recent years.)

Yours sincerely,
M. Polsnok

Polsnok's "chronicle" is *not* a scenario describing what we regard as the most probable development in Sweden in the coming ten years. Thus it must not be thought of as a forecast of probable behavior on the part of the present-day equivalents of the persons appearing in the text. The chronicle is a reference projection, which has been clad in this slightly provocative form in order to make its point more strikingly. It illustrates dynamic properties latent in some of the ideas about international business that prevail in Sweden today. Below we will try to identify, on theoretical and empirical grounds, the conditions that led us to this picture.

(1) There is a risk that because of the differences we have noted in the expectations regarding the future rate of internationalization, the leading part—which probably has most to say on this matter—may leave the lagging groups even further behind. When the gap between expectations and outcome becomes clear to the lagging groups, some type of *reactive* behavior becomes a real possibility. This hypothesis is supported by the comments of the politicians and the trade union leaders on the business executives' plans for the future. (For example; "If things move too quickly, we'll have to try tougher methods, even if they have unfavorable side-effects.)"

(2) All politicians and trade union leaders have to pay attention to the opinions of the voters, and this makes it difficult for an overall view of the

internationalization problematique to become generally accepted. At least that is the view of those who are to be exposed to the judgment of the electorate. Since the decision-makers are far from positive in their view of the voters' ability to understand the problems of internationalization fully, and since they regard the people as nationalistic and selfish, they rather naturally compete for the favor of the voters with projects appealing to nationalistic feeling. As the political game generally allows for short-term planning only, it is not very surprising that the measures proposed are somewhat haphazard in their effects.

(3) The availability of convenient economic-political instruments such as the testing of individual cases encourages short-sighted action. When the consequences of decisions are as obvious as they are when it is simply a question of saying "yes" or "no" to an application to invest abroad, the temptation is great in a difficult situation to look exclusively at the short-run effects, especially at those that can be readily expressed in figures and communicated to others. The factors least likely to be considered are probably developments abroad; on the other hand far too much weight will be given, in overall social-economic terms, to direct local consequences in the decision-makers' own country. And the natural desire of politicians to be elected reinforces the tendency in party-political campaigning to exploit the advantages of the case-by-case approach.

(4) Differences in opinion about the effects of various economic-political measures can easily result in an escalation of restrictions. From the results presented in Chapters 4–6 we can see that in the leading system in the internationalization process, i.e., the corporations, a restrictive and nationalistic policy is regarded as ineffective and possibly even counter-effective. Instead of preventing the outflow of jobs, it leads to the substitution of foreign production for export and to a strategy of loophole-hunting among the restrictions. The larger companies have plenty of experience operating in a heterogeneous environment, often in more difficult conditions than those prevailing in Sweden; it does not, therefore, seem likely that they will suffer much in the ethnocentric world. This view of the multinational corporations as inaccessible to nationally-oriented actions contrasts sharply with the world views of the politicians and the trade union leaders, who almost without exception envisage a good chance of being able to control international business from their home bases. If this confidence proves misplaced —as we have reason to expect that it may—then the companies will be subject to even greater strain, and discriminatory action against other countries will increase. It would probably be difficult to design "neutral" control tools, given the short time that is generally available.

(5) The likelihood of national solutions increases as the chances of international collaboration decline. An international trade union movement would be an effective obstacle to the fragmentation into national units of the trade union element in the global industrial system. If, on the other hand, the trade unions' strategy aims chiefly at exploiting their links with political parties to ensure their position as a restraining force at the national level, then the unions could help to push us towards a world of the Scenario B type. The situation is similar in politics. If international rule systems for the

multinational corporation can be created, it will be very difficult for individual countries to introduce restrictive and discriminatory policies.[2] As well as collaboration in organs such as the UN, OECD and so on, agreements between the major trade blocs are also extremely important in this context. The negotiations between EEC and the USA are of the utmost importance here. A breakdown could easily lead the world towards a regional variant of Scenario B, a "bloc world" almost certainly marred by increasing political tension.

(6) Instances of multinational corporations behaving in such a way as to provoke the nation states can have enormous implications for developments as a whole. Every time a corporation oversteps the mark in some way, vigorous counter-measures are taken in the unstable climate that at present surrounds the whole MNC question. Because business is the leading part in the internationalization process, any decision that underlines or is thought to underline the gap between the corporations and the nationally organized systems risks producing violent reactions from the latter. The element of shock is probably very important here. If the environment is informed in good time of a company's future plans, there is less risk of reactive behavior with subsequent retaliatory and discriminatory consequences. In other words, the very power of the large multinational corporations constitutes a threat to their own existence and, in the long run, to private enterprise as such, since the large MNCs are apparently insensitive to many national economic-political measures. Recognition of this insensitivity can easily encourage the idea that the corporations and society as a whole are necessarily in conflict with one another.

(7) The difficulty involved in trying to determine scientifically the causal relationships of the internationalization problematique deserves a point to itself. Every examination of the effect of internationalization on a particular factor—employment for example—suffers from a fundamental weakness: it has to be based on an *assumption* of what would happen if foreign investment had *not* taken place, and the reasonableness of such assumptions can always be questioned.[3] One might think that the difficulty in agreeing on an assessment of the effects would lead politicians and trade union leaders to be cautious in the assumptions, but in modern social policy the employment problem is sacrosant, which means that arguments often circle round this question despite lack of knowledge and sometimes even lack of relevance to the particular problem. For instance, if we assume that one country's losses in employment as a result of internationalization will be another's gains, it is immaterial from the global economic point of view what the specific effects are (disregarding the costs of structural change in monetary and human terms). In Sweden it was because of the difficulty of evaluating the overall consequences of international business operations that there has been such insistence on the separate evaluation of every project from the "national economic" point of view. A factor which might stabilize such attempts at geographical and sector-wise simplification of the problems is that the possibility of learning by trial-and-error is very slight. Causal relations become even more complex when one of many possible legislation models also has to be included among the explanatory variables.

It is our view that such isolated manifestations of the internationalizations problematique as employment, exchange balance, inflation and regional imbalance should not provide the basis for future planning in this field. The zero-sum game between nations which arises from such a view only serves to turn our attention away from the more essential aspects of the power of the multinational business. Whether we want to describe and analyse future developments in this field or to provide a basis for active planning of the future, a total perspective over the question of internationalization must provide the essential basis.

(8) The complexity of industrial society generates a longing for simplifications. The populist movements that are spreading over Europe today show how large sections of the population are suffering from chronic fatigue; they are tired of the delicate balance between all the demands and interests within and between countries that characterize the economics and the politics of contemporary society. Furthermore, these interdependencies have been administered by an academically educated corps of civil servants who have long been dubbed the "bureaucrats." They often claim openly that they are the only people who fully understand the problems, thus providing the populist reaction with concrete targets. Many political writers have tried to explain "Glistrupism" (after a Danish populist presently having considerable success) and related phenomena as factors specific to the particular country concerned. We believe, instead, that political scientists and sociologists would do well to interpret populism as a reaction towards an increasingly turbulent environment, whose complexity is so great that it automatically generates a need to simplify.[4] This need can express itself in different ways, according to the circumstances in the specific countries at specific points in time, but obviously a growing tendency to insist on a national identity geographically defined is one such simple alternative; the longing to throw off any dependence on decisions made by "strangers" in general is another. One of bureaucracy's strategies is to channel dissatisfaction towards "strangers" and away from itself, and nationalistic strains come readily to hand.

To recapitulate, we have *not made forecast* of the future here; we have provided a definition of the present by projecting it on the future, under the unrealistic assumption that nothing in the system we are studying will change. With the help of the reference projection we can identify the dissonances which exist today, in the hope that we shall be able to avoid them tomorrow. Later we will discuss some dissonance-reducing elements and strategies in the global industrial system, but first something should be said about the extent to which the results and analyses of the Swedish investigation can perhaps provide grounds for conclusions about developments in the world in general.

SWEDEN AS A SOCIAL EXPERIMENTAL LABORATORY

Many behavioral scientists regard the Scandinavian countries in general, and Sweden in particular, as a laboratory where values and behavior which will later appear in a wider context appear for the first time.[5] Arguments that could support this thesis are as follows: *First*, Sweden is *economically a well-developed country*, which is meeting the problems of the post-industrial society earlier than other countries which still have major economic needs to satisfy. *Secondly*, and this excludes many countries which satisfy the first requirement for membership in the group of social laboratories, Sweden is a *small* country with a population which in many respects is very *homogeneous*; this reduces the importance of various "disturbing factors" connected with such issues as race and religion. *Thirdly*, and this is partly connected with the other points but is also explained by history and tradition, the *feedback process between sections of society is very rapid in Sweden*. Most news services are centralized, thus supplying nearly all Sweden with an almost identical basis for discussion. Also, because of the tradition of trying to seek a consensus on all questions, consultation between "opponents" occurs very much more widely in Sweden than in many other countries. Morover, in Sweden there are no social barriers or class discriminations to delay developments such as there are in countries like France, Germany, England and Italy, to mention only a few.

Fourthly, and this is important to our purpose, Sweden is vulnerable to the consequences of the internationalization of business in a way quite unlike that of most other countries. Foreign trade amounts to about 20 percent of the gross national product, compared with about 4 percent in the USA. Sweden houses both foreign MNCs and the parent companies of globally operating Swedish corporations. The state of business activity and, consequently, of employment and economic growth depends to a great extent on conditions in foreign countries. For all these reasons Sweden, much more that many other countries, must regard itself as part of a larger system. Because we believe that technological developments call for a more open and interdependent global economy, we also feel that Sweden can illustrate the situation that will confront many other countries in the future (assuming that there will be technological development in the future).

Our Swedish readers may smile a little at the idea of Sweden as the pioneer going ahead of many much larger countries, but abroad, Sweden is in fact often regarded as an example in miniature of how the future will look.[6] Companies use Sweden as a test market for new products; politicians in France, for example, speak of "the Swedish model;" journalists warn of the technocratic, "corporativist" type of future that is reflected by developments in Sweden. In trade union contexts, the Swedes are willing to pay for international collaboration, and are regarded as an example on the organization front. For Sweden, this means that active planning for the future is even more important, since developments in other nations are dependent on the Swedish reality to an extent that is quite out of proportion to the size of the country. The more immediate implication is that Sweden can use its advantages as a social experimental laboratory to try out alternatives which other countries cannot. The Swedish futures are both more numerous and more open to influence than their equivalents in most of the other industrialized countries.

DISSONANCE-REDUCING ELEMENTS IN THE GLOBAL INDUSTRIAL SYSTEM

What chiefly characterizes the above reference projection is that nobody presumably wants to acknowledge the future it reflects, but that the sum (or rather the *system*) of the actions presented can easily lead to an end state that nobody wants. In other words, in the perceptions of the internationalization problematique that prevail in Sweden and the world today, there are dynamic characteristics that could result in sub-optimal behavior from the Swedish and the world point of view. We are now going to try to identify the factors which militate *against*, or *should* militate against, such a development. From the logic of the reference projection it follows that to a great extent these factors do not exist today, which means that a good deal of speculation and innovation must lie behind many of them. However, we have endeavored to mention only those "solutions" to the dilemma of the reference projection which, in light of the results of our empirical investigation, are *possible* in view of the variety of values, plans and expectations prevailing in society today. Thus, what we are looking for is some form of intersection set between the possible and the ideal. With this starting-point it is possible to use our "critique" of the reference projection as a basis for planning and controlling the Swedish future.

This approach may appear to conflict with our fundamental philosophy as reported in Chapters 2 and 3. We are now taking up *separate* aspects of the problematique, and not suggesting *totalities*, which penetrate the inadequacies of the reference projection. Let us therefore stress that the particularistic form in which we communicate our ideas has nothing to do with the procedure followed in our work. The search for specific partial solutions has been governed by an idea of a total solution (or rather, to use Ackoff's concept, dissolution). The first approximation of such a total solution is represented by Scenario C, as it was presented to our respondents. Our results appear to confirm that this scenario provides a rough picture of a total global future which is perceived as both probable and desirable by large and powerful groups in Swedish society and, consequently, can also supply a first rough sketch for the country's planning for a future in a global industrial system. Further, the theoretical analysis we presented in Chapter 2 results in a world resembling Scenario C as at least *one* possible future. Naturally our own values have governed us in our search for alternatives, but we believe that we stand on much firmer ground here than these alone could supply. Below we discuss some different interrelated dissonance-reducing strategies associated with the global industrial system, after which we will try to place them all in a total picture.

More Rapid Feedback Processes in Society

One of the factors that led to the gloomy end state in the reference projection was that differences in expectations concerning the future were not revealed in time. One way of reducing the risk of sub-optimality and dysfunctionality in the Swedish and the global system, is to *increase the information* to each one of the components in the system about the attitudes, values and plans of the other components. As we saw from the presentation of results in Chapters 4–6, there is a gap between the business executives on the one hand and the politicians and trade union people on the other when it comes to expectations about the rate of internationalization. This confirms the relevance of the concept of the "leading part." At the same time it shows how the multinational corporations "homogenize" the nationally organized systems. As we saw in Chapter 6, party affiliation has no decisive part to play in determining which forecasts politicians make about the scope and character of internationalization. Since it is the business executives who have the greatest influence on the future shape of the companies, there is probably a great risk that the lagging systems will react sharply as developments are actually realized and the information gap is bridged.

We have explained the gap in expectations as stemming from different forecasts of future legislation against international enterprise. Since our results and our theoretical analyses both suggest that the effect of economic-political measures is very limited in this sphere, this explanation should only be used as we have used it, namely as an explanation of the world view of our particular respondents, but *not* as a theory about the actual appearance of reality. It is therefore probable that, if no changes take place, the information gap will manifest itself in future skirmishes, regardless of how restrictive or liberal the policy towards the internationally operating companies is felt to be. Any hope of effectively steering the Swedish future will increase as the people, whose actions determine this future are made aware of their inter-dependencies with each other. Thus, the operation of an active and successful planning system requires further debate about the establishment of Swedish industry on foreign markets—how much, how quickly and in what form. It also requires a further examination of the response of the large corporations to national economic-political measures—how much do they react and in what way. At risk of appearing too pedagogical, in Table 7:1 we have rearranged the results from Chapters 4–6 to reveal even more clearly what we consider to be the most important information gaps (*see* boxes in Table 7:1).

If a dialogue is necessary between different parts of society in order to communicate expectations and plans, it is equally important that the values associated with the internationalization problematique should be clarified and discussed. Ignorance about the intentions of other parties provides a breeding ground for fruitless squabbles about separate parts of reality instead of a constructive debate about the whole of it. The striking but necessarily oversimplified declarations we hear from politicians, trade unions and business should perhaps be replaced by scenarios (after all, scenario-writing is a technique for communicating total pictures) in which the long-term goals and the consequences of a particular policy are described. This would provide an opportunity for criticism of the goals and the envisaged effects. In this way a political party, a company, or a trade union would be compelled to seek some sort of consistency in its actions. It is the short-sighted stopgap actions that lead turbulent systems into dysfunctionality. For this reason *a more open and broader ideological debate* would be extremely valuable.

Table 7:1

	The situation today	In 10 years time[3]	Scenario A	Scenario B	Scenario C
Proportion of sales abroad for Swedish manufacturing companies (percent of total sales)					
Business executives	55[1]	69	69	54	—
LO	55	65	67	52	66
Politicians	55	63	65	50	62
Proportion of production abroad for Swedish manufacturing companies (percent of total production)					
Business executives	17[1]	31	31	29	—
LO	17	23	27	18	24
Politicians	17	24	26	16	21
Proportion of industrial employment in foreign-owned industry in Sweden (percent of total industrial employment)					
Business executives	10	—	—	—	—
LO	10	13	15	10	14
Politicians	10	16	17	10	13
Growth in Swedish manufacturing companies' production over the next 10 years (percent per year)					
Business executives	5.0[2]	8.0	8.0	5.0	—
LO	5.0	5.8	5.9	4.1	5.6
Politicians	5.0	4.7	4.7	3.1	4.8

[1] Unweighted mean value for the Swedish companies interviewed in 1972.
[2] Mean value for the period 1960–1970.
[3] Mean value for all respondents. The evaluations of the business executives concern their *own* companies.

It is particularly interesting for the corporations to note that what rouses negative reactions in political and trade union quarters is not so much the consequences of internationalization as its apparent inaccessibility and tendency to take the various other interested parties by surprise. A more open attitude on the part of the corporations—expressing itself in early information about plans to establish abroad and a willingness to discuss in advance the consequences of alternative projects—would probably give much more room for manoeuvres in the long run and would create a more expansive environment for the corporations than would ever be possible by insisting on the "wise control of the invisible hand." Any company which embarked on a more open dialogue with the rest of society, and which took into account the "external" effects that its actions might have, would almost certainly find itself at a disadvantage in competition in the short run. Common action by all companies, or the application of rules accepted by them all, is, therefore, almost a precondition for the successful operation of a strategy of "waiting for" the lagging systems. It is in this sense that agreements in the International Chamber of Commerce,[7] for example, can be very valuable, while any attempt to design all-embracing rule systems for companies international operations within the frameworks of business enterprise is fruitless. The organizations that feel threatened by the rapid spread of the multinationals will certainly not hand over the responsibility for legislation to those whom they wish to legislate against. They would prefer to have at least some say themselves.

The research project "Futures of Sweden" is an attempt to create a dialogue between different parts of Swedish society. At the same time, one of the findings of the project is that an even quicker feedback of information and evaluations is necessary. To satisfy this demand we need both a willingness on the part of all parties to enter into discussion and new platforms for the exchange of opinions and information. We will not embark here on a detailed discussion of how these new institutions should be designed, but will simply indicate the change in established organizational forms to which they may give rise in the long run. Thus, the chief obstacle to the creation of new information channels seems to be the sluggishness that characterizes all large organizations. As we mentioned in Chapter 2, the immediate future is going to make great demands on the ability of institutions to renew themselves, to try out new forms of organization and strategies, and perhaps even to erase their own former identities. This general rule for acting in complex environments can also be applied to the more restricted problem of increasing the contact spaces between those taking part in the creation of the future of the global industrial system.

Internationalization of the Corporation's Stakeholders

The most powerful obstacle to a nationalistic future would be an internationalization of the political and trade union organs. Organizations which acknowledge responsibility for a global system do not pursue policies by which all individual nations would lose in the long run. The nationalistic policy is generally regarded, particularly in the Swedish trade union movement, as by and large a regrettable *second-best alternative* to an internationalistic line. For this reason all Swedish political and trade union organs should work forcefully for international solutions. Companies, particularly small ones (and most Swedish companies are small ones), also gain in the long run from an *internationalization of the stakeholder system* in their environment.

As we have mentioned before, the Swedish trade union movement is very positive towards the idea of trade union collaboration across national frontiers. Nevertheless, difficulties in the shape of political and religious schisms between and within nations make it seem pretty unlikely that it will be possible to achieve very much in this direction in the near future. Greater flexibility in the forms assumed by trade union internationalism would probably help to ease the birth pangs. Emphasis on the company and branch level would probably be particularly effective, although the big organizational changes this would require at the national central level would be an obstacle to such a development (*see* Chapter 5); once again the call for new institutions and the dismantling of old ones would make the power-holders in the traditional organizations hesitate. Fear of the labels that might attach to the kind of "staff clubs" that could result from a far-reaching decentralization of trade union work at the international level is quite understandable. However, it should be possible to find or invent forms for collaboration between local and central levels which would reduce the risk of channeling the working class struggle into support for one company against others and for one historically favoured group of nations against the underprivileged countries. As the Western European trade union movement acquires influence over the multinational corporations, it will also, to a much greater extent and in a more concrete way, acquire responsibility for distributing the good things of the earth between the nations. This will call for specific decisions about global income distribution; it will be more difficult to blame economic laws for differences in wealth.

We will not discuss in any great detail here the different models or examples of trade union internationalism, but refer the interested reader to the literature available in this sphere.[8]

Political organs find it even more difficult than trade union organs to collaborate internationally. Most observers, including our respondents, are very gloomy about the outlook for achieving a uniform system of rules for the multinational corporations by means of political decisions. Such general guidelines as can be achieved through international negotiations must necessarily be formulated in extremely vague terms; no real sanctions are possible, since the different countries have such a variety of interests to watch over. The importance of the codes of behavior lies rather in that they probably help to reduce the feeling of powerlessness felt by many politicians in relation to the multinational corporations, since at least the rudiments of a restraining political power at the international level can appear to symbolize a change in power relations. Furthermore, the emergence of international institutions does provide an opportunity for a more thorough debate of the MNC problematique. The least that can emerge from the work of the UN committee dealing with this question is probably some form of information centre, to which governments—mainly the governments of the developing countries—can turn for information about specific companies, for advice in negotiations, for access to economic expertise, and so on. This means that the feedback process between the different parts of the global industrial system is administered at an international level. This is a good thing in itself; it also helps in the long run to create an atmosphere in which a more far-reaching political internationalism could grow.

The diversity of the conditions prevailing in different parts of the world motivates the use of more limited models for government collaboration than those used by the United Nations. Regional associations of nations have already put extensive sets of rules into operation, and for the developing countries the Andean Pact model represents a probable, and presumably also a desirable, future. The risk of a regional variant of the regulatory world is that tensions between blocs of nations can easily arise. Nevertheless, it is probably necessary that the obvious differences between the rich and the poor countries find expression in somewhat differentiated systems for the control of the multinational corporations. In the longer term the increasing importance of the developing countries in the world economy as suppliers of raw material and as markets may lead to global solutions. Thus the most urgent question today is to see that the systems applied in the industrialized and the developing countries are not so unlike as to obstruct their ultimate combination. To this must be added that an effective control of the actions of the MNCs in the developing countries exerted by these countries themselves would involve a comparative loss of welfare in the industrialized world. For this reason government-level contacts between the countries will ultimately be necessary to negotiate an acceptable distribution of the good things of this world. Negotiations of this kind should not be allowed to develop into a battle between individual nations for the favors of the raw-material-supplying developing countries; they should rather be conducted at an international level. Consequently it is very important to reach an agreement on how to deal with the global interdependencies in the industrialized world, if severe political tension is to be avoided in the future. From the narrow national point of view, of course, we could claim that provided the struggle stopped short of military conflict, Sweden would probably manage relatively well in a world of bilateral nation-administered internationalism.

Participation in the Internationalization Process at the Grassroots Level

It was characteristic of the reference projection that, in order to strengthen their own positions or those of their organizations, decision-makers exploited and appealed to the voters' supposed "Swedishness" and narrow partial interests. They even tried to satisfy the normal human longing for a more or less comprehensible environment by designating foreign scapegoats for the misfortunes that Sweden suffered in the way of unemployment, for example. There are two ways of avoiding the escalation of nationalistic fevers that would be the result of a political struggle in terms such as these.

First, efforts can be made to cleanse the political debate of the use of nationalistic tricks. Although most high-ranking politicians and most trade union leaders do generally reject arguments based on simplifications and easy appeals to nationalistic sentiments, nevertheless the temptation to win political advantage by the use of such methods is probably too great to rely solely on the self-discipline of those in power. Also, of course, the call for drastic action does not come only from tactical strategists in the top echelons of society; it seems to have its foremost adherents at the local level in the organizations (*see* Chapters 5 and 6).

The second way of avoiding the mechanisms of the reference projection is therefore to make "the people" immune to propaganda of a nationalistic and particularistic nature. It is a question of getting ordinary wage-earners to look at the internationalization problems from an overall viewpoint, and the most effective way of doing this is to give the ordinary wage-earner more direct influence over decisions concerning internationalization. Representation on the boards of directors naturally calls for a deeper analysis of the company's situation, in which international operations are seen as part — and sometimes as a precondition — of Swedish operations. However, this is not enough. A company board owes its primary responsibility to those who are directly affected by its activities, including the employees. It has less responsibility, however, to Swedish society as a whole and less still to the world. If the voice of the grassroots in society is to be heard when major economic decisions about internationalization are being made, the gaps between the hierarchies in the political parties and in the wage-earner organizations must be reduced. In Chapter 5 we showed how ideas about the multinational corporations diverge between the central and the local levels of the trade union movement. If these differences are not to exert pressure from below, compelling the top organs to fall back on popular nationalistic and restrictive measures, it will be necessary to intensify the dialogue in the Swedish trade union movement about international enterprise. If no definite overall picture can be found that is acceptable to all ranks in the organizations, then the door is open to anyone wanting to use particularist weapons in his own interests. Naturally a dialogue of this sort in the trade union movement would affect the stability of the system, but it is surely better for the wage-earner organizations if the gaps are revealed now when something can perhaps be done to fill them, rather than coming as a shock when there won't be any time for farsighted deliberations.

At the same time, an intensification of the political debate should help to protect individual citizens from succumbing to simplified nationalistic arguments. It is particularly important that those who design the overriding policy on the international mobility of business should not be labeled "bureaucrats" or "technocrats." The responsibility for preventing populist reactions falls, of course, on the "bureaucrats" themselves in the first instance. They must make every effort to present their ideas about long-term policies comprehensibly so that ordinary people can understand them and, perhaps even more important, can have a chance to formulate and communicate their own views about them.[9] It seems to us that the assessment of individual applications for investment permission in the Currency Exchange Control Board which has been suggested by the Special Committee (and which has now been approved by and large by the Riksdag and put into effect) will make it more difficult to tackle questions more fundamental than the employment situation in one community or another. The case method is meant to make it easier to assess the total effects of internationalization. But from the point of view of national economics and, even more, of world economics, a disproportionate emphasis on the effects of individual cases can have unfortunate consequences. If this type of readily available instrument is to be effective, then there must first be some sort of total view to provide a base for the separate decisions. If such a basic view does exist, then the case method is a convenient tool; if no such view exists, the method is dangerous. For this reason the Special Committee, which at the time of writing is still operating, should now concentrate on the more fundamental issues associated with the emergent global industrial system. In particular it should see that debate on this question spreads to and beyond the "lowest" levels in Swedish political life.

New Coalitions, Forms of Collaboration and Institutions

These three strategies for planning in a complex environment all call for a revision of existing organizational and operational patterns. What new forms of interaction could evolve in a system increasingly global in character? We do not wish to overload the text with references to our interview results, but the reader can confirm the support these provide for our suggestions by turning back to Chapters 4–6.

For the Nations

The driving-force behind the emergence of a regulatory world such as that described in Scenario C is an increase in direct state participation in the process of internationalization. This is *not* the same as internationalizing the political system in the world; rather it reflects a pattern of behavior among national governments that is more aggressive than would be warranted by trying to keep internationalization under control. As we see it, international agreements cannot replace the more spontaneous structures that are generated as the state takes a more active part in supranational industrial operations, but they could very well provide an extremely important complement to such structures. The main task of the international conventions is to prevent state-administered internationalism from generating a politicially labile "bloc" world; but it is doubtful whether they have a role to play as regulators of the privately owned MNCs. In Chapter 2 we discussed in some detail the arguments for and against an increase in state intervention, so it is unnecessary to repeat these here. It can be seen from the findings reported in Chapters 5 and 6 that strong trade union and political forces are working in this direction, which supports the theoretical argument presented in Chapter 2.

The most obvious form of state participation is represented by an increase in ownership or influence in domestic companies with international operations. There are many examples of at least partially state-owned multinational corporations, among which the oil company British Petroleum (BP) is perhaps the best known. A great many more such corporations will almost certainly see the light of day in the future, because so much capital will be needed and so much importance will be attached to the corporations in the national economies, that state participation will be found necessary. This development will probably not be politically controversial, since industrial leaders and socialists (in Sweden, at any rate, the Social Democrats) will be able to agree on the value of individual projects while differing in their ideas about the ultimate direction of the tendency. An important consequence of this kind of state commitment is that the anxiety at home about internationalization dies down. As the state takes upon itself to participate actively in controlling the internationalization process, the kind of demands that are heard today from trade union and political interests for evaluations in terms of the national economy are more or less automatically satisfied. At least it probably feels as though such evaluations are being made. In fact, as we have mentioned before, it is extremely difficult to make, in any sense, "correct" assessments of the effects of the internationalization process. The usual model, at least in the short run, in the nations that are receiving foreign investment is the company owned jointly by state and private interests. If the fourth Pension Fund[10] in Sweden is systematically used to buy shares in Swedish-owned MNCs, this type of international institution could quickly come to have great importance in the Swedish situation. It would also immediately force the debate about internationalization into new and broader tracks.

The world's governments also have a role to play in representing the host countries. The most immediate development on this front at present is that the demands from the developing countries for national ownership and national management of the multinational corporations' local subsidiaries are going to be much more stringent. This development is in fact already in full swing, regardless of the political ideology of the governments concerned. In the industrialized world, too, it seems likely that there will be an increase in state participation in foreign MNCs—or at least in the influence exerted over their activities. In Sweden the demands on foreign companies are clearly going to be much stricter than before, but our interviews suggest that the social democratic government at least claims not to have any discriminatory intent. The Emmaboda-St. Gobain case illustrates the kind of approach that any Swedish government over the next ten years will probably have to take in its policies towards foreign MNCs. It is interesting to note that the Emmaboda case has been regarded by foreign experts as a proof of Sweden's nondiscriminatory attitude.[11]

These two simple forms of state participation in the internationalization of industry, particularly when they are combined in one and the same company, suggests that the whole MNC issue is being raised to a higher level than when the state remains as a passive participant in the game, reacting and adjusting to events after they have happened. The situation changes even more when the mainly bilateral links become multilateral.

If various states have interests in a single corporation, this can then be designated as a *multinational* in the true sense, rather than as a national corporation with *international* operations. This should help to tone down the picture of the MNC as the extended arm of a particular state—a picture that gives rise to a certain amount of anxiety. In the larger countries this anxiety

may be reinforced when single states increase their influence in the corporations. In the long run, however, multinationalism should find its justification
in the very fact that states and not individual interests are creating the
supranational structure.

Yet another form for a broader type of multinationalism is to be found
in the rapid increase in the number and size of multi-state collaborative
projects, particularly in the research field. State-owned and private companies
from many countries often participate in this kind of project together. It is
very important to see that the process does not stagnate at a bilateral stage,
and some internationalization of the political system—even on a fairly
limited scale—is, therefore, almost essential if state-administrated internationalism is not to lead to a world of conflicting blocs (see Chapter 2 for
a more detailed discussion of these problems).

For the Trade Union Movement

The consequences of trade union influence or even ownership in
multinational companies will be much the same as in the case of state
participation. We have discussed above the transformation of the internationalization problematique that follows from an extension of wage-earner
responsibility into the multinational sphere. We can, therefore, turn immediately to a discussion of possible forms that international business
operations may assume in the future.

For the Companies

Traditionally companies have become international by advancing from
sales-agent to sales-subsidiary status, and then by expanding into production
in foreign countries as well. For much the same reasons that states are
becoming engaged as active partners in multinational business, companies
too are now beginning to divide ownership and resources among themselves. They may share the ownership of subsidiaries with national or
international operations, they may enter into licensing agreements or short-
term collaboration on specific projects, they may agree to share markets or
development assignments, and so on. The number of possible organizational
forms seems to be increasing all the time, and companies need flexibility in
their strategies more than ever before. The term generally used for this type
of collaboration is the *joint venture*, but as this expression has usually been
applied to two-company agreements only and does not distinguish between
different types of organizations, we need some new concepts in this area.
Howard V Perlmutter has coined the term "industrial systems constellation"
to designate the interdependencies underlying the trend towards inter-
company collaboration as well as the diverse forms that such collaboration
can assume. Depending on the geographical situation of the contracting
parties, we can speak of Global Industrial Systems Constellations (GISCs),
Regional Industrial Systems Constellations (RISCs), or National Industrial
Systems Constellations (NISCs). Perlmutter touches upon the possibility
of including state-owned companies in constellations but does not develop
this idea further.[12]

We would like to suggest a classification of existing and possible forms of collaboration in the global industrial system, starting from the geographical and the organizational distance between the components. Our hypothesis is that the acting units in the global industrial system gradually transform themselves (a) from being nationally based to being *multinationally based* and (b) from being rooted in one type of organization and representing one group's interests to being rooted *in diverse organizations and representing many groups' interests.* Figure 7:2 below describes graphically how we imagine this process will evolve.[13]

The broad arrow shows how the increase in global interdependencies forces the emergence of new forms of organization. (The reference projection shows how this trend can be broken by factors favoring a simplification of the interdependencies. But we should repeat yet again that the purpose of the reference projection was to identify the situation in the present, not to provide a forecast.) To show more clearly how the examples we have given of specific institutions fit into the model in Figure 7:2 we can simplify the latter below, dividing each of the two scales in the figure into two extreme categories (*see* Table 7:3).

The suggested dissonance-reducing strategies suggested in this chapter are mainly intended to make it easier to move from the lower left to the upper right corner of Table 7:3. The main problem lies in organizational inertia, which is the chief cause of the kind of relapses we saw in the reference projection. If the transformations in the global industrial system are to be as painless as possible, *each one* of the parties involved will have to show their willingness to sacrifice sovereignty and power; they must also be prepared to share a growing area of responsibility with previous opponents, to make use jointly of the available resources, and to sacrifice short-term and/or self-serving advantages for the sake of the whole group and the future. This will make quite new demands on the men and women appointed to lead the

Figure 7:2

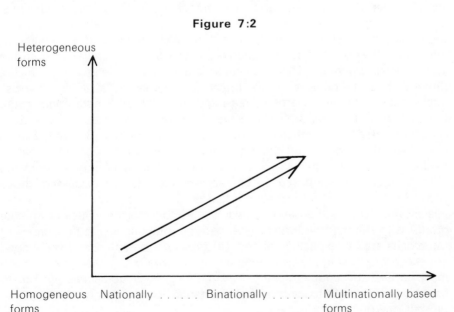

Table 7:3

	Nationally based forms	Multinationally based forms
Heterogeneous forms	Company financing from public funds Tripartite planning organ (government, wage-earner associations and company) Wage-earners on company boards Combined state-private companies	International tripartite type of planning organ ICFTU representatives in MNC's management Wage-earner ownership in MNC's parent company Wage-earner ownership in MNC's subsidiaries State-ownership in MNC's parent company State-ownership in MNC's subsidiaries
Homogeneous	Governments Company mergers, NISCs Trade union central organs State-owned companies Private companies	Global rule system within EEC, UN GISCs, multistate-owned MNCs, ICFTU State-owned MNC Privately-owned MNC

institutions operating in the increasingly complex environment that has been engendered by the removal, as a result of technological developments, of national boundaries and barriers between political, economic and social parts of reality. The future is going to call for considerable personal *integrity*, cultural and social *flexibility, broad knowledge, sensitivity* to changes in values, ability to *learn* quickly from experience and to *question* one's own and other peoples activities—and the demands will apply equally to ministers, business administrators and trade union representatives. Furthermore, organizations must be permeated with a willingness and an ability to regenerate themselves and to undertake active policy-formulation from the lowest levels upwards. This is because the overshadowing danger in the future that can be glimpsed in the upper right corner of Table 7:3 is the risk implicit in the move towards increasingly powerful and more complicated organizations of a *"corporativist" world governed by an élite.* The invectives so often hurled at the officials of the EEC headquarters in Brussels give us some idea of the violent reactions that the concentration of futures-creation to the central and higher levels can arouse in the smaller units whom the "bureaucrats" are supposed to be representing. As we discussed above (pp. 138–139) the main protection against such reactions (and, of course, against the dangers that lie in exposing the world to the values of an elite group) is to see that the fundamental assumptions underlying the actions of top organs are (a) explicitly defined, (b) generally accepted, and (c) shaped at *grass-roots level* in the world community. A *continuous* dialogue between the elite and the people is necessary if the general guidelines are not to become so diluted as to lack any real substance, like the party programmes of present-day politics for instance.

Table 7:4

| | Probability | | | Desirability | | |
	Scenario A	Scenario B	Scenario C	Scenario A	Scenario B	Scenario C
Business executives	2.3	2.8	3.3	3.7	1.4	3.6
LO	2.7	2.2	2.9	2.7	2.0	4.3
Politicians	2.7	1.8	2.8	3.3	1.4	4.0

(Scale 1–5: 1 = not at all probable/desirable; 5 = very probable/desirable.)
All estimates were made during or immediately after the oil crisis, i.e., during November 1973–February 1974.

SWEDEN'S ROLE IN A REGULATED WORLD ECONOMY

Our criteria for effective dissonance-reducing strategies in a turbulent and global industrial system were that the strategies should be both feasible and desirable, and that together they should constitute a consistent whole. Our findings suggest that a world resembling Scenario C, which can be seen as a synthesis of the dissonance-reducing factors discussed above, describes a future that substantial groups in Swedish society regard as relatively probable and desirable. To many influential organizations and persons the scenario appears to represent a sort of intersection set between the possible and the ideal. Table 7:4 shows how the politicians, the trade union leaders and the business executives rank the probability and desirability of the three scenarios. Since Scenario C had not yet been designed when we interviewed the executives the first time, we let a group of about thirty members of a management course represent the executives in the table. It is perhaps worth mentioning, too, that further rankings have since been obtained from similar groups during 1973, 1974, 1975 and 1976, and the results have been similar every time.

As can be seen, Scenario C is regarded as the most probable future by all groups. And to the business executives, who admit to the least sympathy with this type of world, it is almost as desirable as the liberal Scenario A. In interpreting the answers of the business executives, we must make one reservation. The figures are based on the answers of relatively young business leaders—average age a little over forty—of whom the majority are not their company's chief executive. However, the swing in attitude towards a regulated world economy has taken place surprisingly quickly in Swedish industrial circles. When the first business executive interviews were held at the beginning of 1973, a future mainly liberal in character was forecast and expectations of structural and qualitative change were very modest. The way the forecasts have changed, and even more significantly the way *evaluations* of the internationalization process have changed, highlights the special position that Sweden seems to occupy as a greenhouse for social learning and adaptation processes. Our American sister study has revealed far greater conflict between subsystems and much more inertia in the action frameworks than we have found in the Swedish study. Clearly conditions do exist in Swedish society for effective goal-formulation (in the wide sense of the word) for futures planning. The rough outline provided by Scenario C seems to us to provide a starting-point for further dialogue about the administration of the internationalization of Swedish industry and about Sweden's long-term goals for action in international contexts. Also, together with other findings from our study, it provides grounds for identifying areas where Swedish industry can be expected to find a basis for developing internationally competitive competences.

ACTION PROGRAMME FOR COMPANIES, TRADE UNIONS AND POLITICIANS IN SWEDEN

We have tried to describe in rather general terms the changes that we believe to be necessary if unsuitable and from all points of view ineffective "solutions" to the internationalization problematique are to be avoided. Our arguments apply, we believe, at least to the industrialized countries. We subscribe to the belief that the Scandinavian countries provide an indicator of social processes that are still latent in most other countries (*see* p. 131ff). Various manifestations of the problems are at present more apparent in Sweden than in other countries and the opportunity for examining the problems more closely is therefore also greater there. For this reason, and because our analysis is based to a great extent on the results of the Swedish empirical investigation, we would now like to suggest in rather more specific terms action programmes for the three Swedish subsystems studied in this book. Of course, we do not claim to be offering the best action package. On the other hand, we do believe that the direction in which our suggestions point is the right one, and further discussion about ways of achieving the goal would be extremely valuable.

The Companies' Strategy

As we see it, the internationally operating Swedish companies, in particular the large ones, should act in the following way in order to survive and flourish in the global industrial system:

Develop a unique competence for working in and administering complex organizations and other forms of collaboration, particularly such as include foreign interests and consist of heterogeneous parts.

Concentrate their efforts on working out *total solutions* to large problems.

Seek knowledge and experience of work on the Eastern European and developing markets. (This is because Swedish industry probably has comparative advantages vis-à-vis other countries' industry in this area. Western Europe will naturally remain the dominant market.)

Direct management training towards providing broad cultural and political knowledge and a sensitivity to the requirements of work in varied and even foreign environments.

Adapt control systems so that parts of a company can fulfill the needs of local markets by developing sensitivity to local conditions specific to the country.

Be prepared to see the operations of their companies incorporated into the national planning of other countries.

Avoid seeking complete control over resources; share instead of own resources.

Support the internationalization of the trade union movement and all attempts to achieve a global code system for international business.

Show great openness in planning and in action towards domestic and foreign stakeholders.

Engage openly in the social and political debate; try not to succumb to partisan arguments.[14]

Admittedly, not all these points involve revolutionary new thinking. Many companies already behave in several of the ways we suggest. In fact, their example shows that these ideas do represent possible strategies for Swedish companies, at least in the short run. And we believe that these strategies for Swedish industry are the best strategies with which to face the environmental conditions depicted in Scenario C or those in the ethnocentric Scenario B. Sweden should retain at least some chance of acting independently in a protectionist world. An extremely liberal development, such as that described in Scenario A, might appear to give more room for manoeuvres to companies than we have suggested above, but harsh exploitation of the advantages offered by a mainly passive environment would soon result in violent reactions of the type outlined in the reference projection. Thus it seems to us that the companies' most sensible strategy in the long run should be one that is adapted to a world that they have actively helped to create and one in which their previous opponents gradually become their collaborative partners (and vice versa).

The Trade Unions' Strategy

The trade unions should:

Do everything possible to create effective and active international trade union cooperation.

Remain flexible as regards the forms of international cooperation. Encourage local initiative in particular.

Concentrate their efforts on designing long-term action programmes. Avoid being too absorbed by single cases.

Educate experts on international organizations, both multinational business and international trade union cooperation.

Reject nationalistic arguments, even if in the short run they might favour Swedish wage-earner interests.

Persuade corporate management to give full information in good time about plans to expand abroad.

Initiate debates at the local level within the trade union movement about Sweden's problems and opportunities in a global economy.

Let policies be designed at the local levels; avoid above all the concentration of all knowledge and opinion-building to a few people only.

Work for wage-earner representation on company boards, even in foreign subsidiaries, whenever this is legally possible.

Through the local branches, demand insight into the operations and plans of the parent company of foreign corporations established in

Sweden. Establish contact with the trade unions in these companies' home countries.

Strengthen the collaboration between the central Swedish trade union organizations dealing with internationalization questions. In the long run their interests are identical.

Be prepared for rapid changes in organizations and operational forms. Increase flexibility within the movement.

Regard the system of negotiations as changeable. See that national wage negotiations are coordinated with negotiations abroad.

Encourage and initiate discussions with business leaders and capital-owners about the future of Swedish industry.

Bring up questions concerning the developing countries at the local level and let the principles guiding policy towards these countries be decided at the grass-roots level. Have confidence in the members of the movement.

Intensify contacts with Eastern European trade unions, but be prepared for big difficulties.

Strive for wage-earner ownership in the Swedish multinational corporations.

The Politicians' Strategy
The politicians should:

Avoid all nationalistic tones like the plague. Aim at agreement between the parties not to risk a mounting wave of "Swedishness" as a short-sighted vote-winning argument. Make it quite clear that Sweden is dependent on her relations with other countries.

Strive to formulate and determine a total view and a long-term action programme for policies in the global industrial system.

Regard the review of applications for investment abroad in the Currency Exchange Control Board as a channel for information and discussion, rather than a court procedure.

Support all attempts to introduce internationally applicable rules for multinational corporations.

Pursue a policy favorable to the developing countries, it will pay in the long run. Increase aid to the developing countries substantially, but avoid "tied" aid. Work for completely untied aid in international organs.

Seek cooperation with private companies for large projects abroad, particularly in the developing countries and the Eastern countries. Make it quite clear to other countries that restrictions on the multinational corporations in Sweden are not discriminatory. Clearly define guidelines for policy towards foreign-owned companies. In particular, demand full information in good time about buying or investment plans. Seek representation on the boards of directors and, in the longer run, part ownership in the companies.

Discuss internationalization more thoroughly within the political parties. See that experts are confronted with the voters. Intensify the debate on principles and ideologies.

Encourage discussions between business people, politicians and trade union people about internationalization.

Work for the constructive use of public funds to support successful companies operating internationally. Avoid using the pension funds, for example, as a buffer against employment or for capital investment purposes.

Try to remain outside any possible trade wars. Avoid all increases in tariffs and other barriers to trade; distinguish between trade policy and control of MNCs.

Educate experts on questions of trade, reinforce the commercial and economic surveillance of the "state-trading" countries.

This set of strategies and lines of action in the global industrial system is adapted, both in the passive and the active sense, mainly to a regulatory world such as that described in Scenario C. In other words the strategies provide a driving force for such a development as well as way of adjusting to it. Since conditions beyond Sweden's boundaries to a great extent control the future, it is important that the Swedish action programme should not flounder on dysfunctionalities with other environmental assumptions. We believe that the above recommendations fulfill this requirement. In a protectionist world these strategies—the nondiscriminatory policy and state of relative nonalignment to economic blocs, the concentration on developing countries and Eastern markets, and the development of free trade with the EEC—all provide safeguards against the serious consequences for the country's economy that would follow an escalation of restrictions. An extremely liberal world may appear unfavorable to a Swedish policy according to the above. However, it is our conviction that such strong forces are working against such a future, that possible losses in the short run will be more than outweighed by the long-term advantages of early experience of interorganizational discussion and planning and protection against external effects—such as environmental pollution, trash culture and reification.

SUMMARY

The reference projection has shown us that expectations, values and plans prevailing in Sweden today are dysfunctional to solving the internationalization problematique. The present contains dissonances which could result in an undesirable development in the future. In this chapter we have identified and described these dissonances and suggested some dissonance-reducing elements and strategies. These are supported by our results and by theoretical arguments. Together they represent a consistent picture of a society actively striving for and adapting to a future in which international enterprise is no longer a problem to be *solved*, but a problematique that is "automatically" *dissolved.*[16]

For large groups of influential Swedes the vision of a whole represented in very rough outline by Scenario C offers a synthesis of the possible and the ideal. This scenario is generally regarded as the development towards which we will ultimately tend, regardless of what we do today. However, the recommended dissonance-reducing elements are not forecasts; they represent a set of possible courses of action that together constitute an action package in an *interactive* planning process. As well as indicating a *pro*active attitude towards the future this interactivity extends to relations between organizations in Sweden and to relations between Sweden and other countries.[17] Sweden has been marked out as a nation with unique opportunities for studying and identifying the internationalization problematique and for actively steering its own future. This is what gives our analysis international relevance. (Apart from what was said above, pp. 131–132, it would probably not have been possible to carry out a project such as the "Futures of Sweden" in many other countries, because of the generally negative attitude of decision-makers to action research at the societal level.) Taking the results of our interviews as a base, we have therefore worked out specific action programmes for the actors in the Swedish enclave of the global industrial system. The total action package is adapted to a global future such as that depicted in Scenario C, but it is also functional in a protectionist and, in the longer term, in a liberal world. *Neither our recommendations nor the over-arching total picture are to be regarded as final; instead, their function is to provoke and stimulate intensified debate about Sweden's future in a complex international environment.*

It could be said that the "Futures of Sweden" study has arrived not at at a forecast of Sweden's future, but at a series of statements beginning ". . . it depends on." What "it" depends on has been identified, and a number of *conditions* for achieving a non-desired as well as a desired state have been described. The critical factors that determine Sweden's future can perhaps best be described as four *rifts or gaps between and within organizations.*

First, we have the gap in expectations, values and plans *between different types of institutions within individual countries.* This gap is exemplified by the diverging forecasts of the future of Swedish industry between trade union and political decision-makers on the one hand, and business executives on the other. Another example is the very different perceptions of reality entertained in the USA by trade unions and the administration.

The second gap is the one *between similar organizations in different countries.* Perhaps the most important example is the split within the trade union movement. But the inability of the politicians to achieve uniform rules for the MNCs and the different way that Swedish and American business leaders view their respective opponents also deserve to be mentioned. Also, because they compete with one another, the companies themselves cannot always be said to have identical interests.

Thirdly, there is a gap *between central and local levels within specific types of organization* in specific countries. The relatively positive attitude of the top trade union officials towards a liberal future compared with the attitude of the shop stewards was one example. Another was that departmental officials in the government and the rank-and-file of the Riksdag had quite different ideas about the rate at which Swedish business would become internationalized. There was also an internal conflict in the business world, where small businessmen had quite a different attitude towards politicians compared with the representatives of big business.

If they are not to result in tensions of potential danger to Sweden as a whole, all these gaps must be bridged by information, changes in values, and new institutions. Sweden has unique opportunities to accomplish this, but a forth gap is thereby revealed: namely, the gap *between the elite and the organizations on the one hand and the "people" and individual members of the public* on the other. If the conflicts in and between the large powerful organizations are solved by means of intensified dialogue and the assumption of wider areas of responsibility by different institutions in consort, then there is a great risk that individual people feel (and in fact are!) powerless. The result could be either a purely corporativist state (or even world), or a world full of enormous tension which could have highly uncertain results. Sweden is probably one of the countries in which a corporativist development has come closest, since the consensus idea is widespread among those in positions of power and accepted by public opinion to an extent without parallel in the rest of the western world.[18]

NOTES

1. Cf. H. Ozbekhan, "Thoughts on the Emerging Methodology of Planning," *mimeograph* 1973, where the method used in this chapter of revealing dissonances and consonances in the present by means of a reference projection is described.
2. Cf. *Business International Special Supplement*, March 26, 1974, pp. 6–10, in which both the MNCs and the nation's authorities and trade unions are advised to cooperate for their common weal and to sacrifice their individual sovereignty.
3. For examples of studies of the effect on employment at home of foreign establishments, *see* S. H. Ruttenberg, "Needed: A Constructive Foreign Trade Policy." Washington D. C.: AFL-CIO, 1971; *The Impact of US Foreign Direct Investment on US Employment and Trade: An Assessment of Critical and Legislative Proposals.* National Foreign Trade Council, Inc., N.Y., 1971; R. B. Stobaugh, *et.al.* US *Multinational Enterprises and the US Economy.* Boston, Mass., January, 1972.
4. F. E. Emery, and F. L. Trist, *Towards a Social Ecology—Contextual Appreciations of the Future in the Present.* London, N.Y.: Plenum Press, 1973, pp. 57–67.
5. *Emery and Trist, Towards a Social Ecology,* pp. 207–08.
    L. N. Lindberg, "A Prospectus for Political Futures: The Theory and Practice of Post-Industrial Society," University of Wisconsin, unpublished manuscript.
6. On the other hand it has been claimed by political scientists that the very homogeneity of Swedish society renders the debate on societal development more inadequate and less varied than in the continental European countries.

7. "Guidelines for International Investment." *International Chamber of Commerce*, No. 272. Paris 1972.

8. *See*, for example, C. Levinson, "Fackföreningsrörelsen och de Multinationella Företagen." ("The Trade Union Movement and the Multinational Corporations") *Världspolitikens Dagsfrägor 12/1972*, Utrikespolitiska Institutet, Stockholm, 1972; K. Levinson, and P. Sanden, *Kapitalets International. Om de Multinationella Företagen och deras Makt över Människor och Länder* (*The International of Capital: On the Multinational Corporations and their Power over People and Countries*). Stockholm: Prisma Publishers, 1972.

9. The Swedish government's ambition to get various large groups in the country discussing the national long-term energy policy is an example of this kind of measure.

10. The Pension Fund is divided into four parts, each with a separate board. The Fourth Fund is permitted to buy shares.

11. *See Business Europe*, pp. 113–14, 1974.

12. H. V. Perlmutter, "The Multinational Firm and the Future." *The Annals of the American Academy of Political and Social Science*, (September) 1972, pp. 139–52.

13. Cf. the three stages in the future of the global industrial system discussed by Perlmutter, "The Multinational Firm, *op. cit.*, p. 142.

14. The initiative mentioned in note 6 on the part of ICC is a constructive example of an activity that is compatible with this point.

15. This point is discussed in K. Levinson, "Multinationella Företag och Internationella Kollektivavtalsförhandlingar" ("Multinational Corporations and International Collective Bargaining"), in Vahlne (ed.), *Företagsekonomisk Forskning om Internationellt Företagande* (*Business Economic Research on International Enterprising*), Stockholm: Norstedts Publishers, 1974.

16. Ackoff uses the concepts "solve" and "dissolve" to distinguish between partial problem-solving and the penetration of a mess.

17. We are aware that we use the concept of interactive planning in a sense that somewhat from Ackoff's (1974). By and large, however, our interpretations of the concept are commensurate. We have taken *inter*activity to refer not only to the relationship between present activities and the future, but also between organizations and people in the present. Ackoff (1974) sees "integration" and "coordination" as ingredients in interactive planning, which means our use does not do too much violence to the concept. As mentioned above, we were inspired to conceptualize the alternative scenarios in terms of planning attitudes by Ackoff (1972), and all the credit for the concept development work accrues to him.

18. Huntford sees this attribute as the major distinguishing feature of Swedish society as a whole. R. Huntford, *Det Blinda Sverige* (*The New Totalitarians*), Stockholm: Tema 1973.

Postscript and Prologue
HOWARD V. PERLMUTTER

The critical issue for Sweden must be, given the evolution of the global industrial system, to what degree will the Sweden of tomorrow be permitted to improve its quality of living and maintain the social and political values Swedes cherish? What new global values will emerge and intrude into the institutional life of Sweden as a function of Sweden's increasing dependence on the world economy? What preparedness do Sweden's institutions, like government, business, and labor, have to face a global future? Sweden as a small, technologically advanced, social welfare-oriented, homogenous and neutral state in a Global Industrial System has strengths the vast majority of small and large nations do not have. The statistical indices will demonstrate these strengths: Educational level, social objectives, level of employment, level of technology. What may not be widely recognized is that the quality and abundance in Swedish life depends in part on firms with multinational interests. These Swedish firms who expand globally recognize that host country stakeholders from all over the world will become more vocal. "By what right," a host political leader may ask, "does this Swedish company use our resources, generate almost as much profits in our country as the home country, use our people as employees, depend on our customers, borrow from our banks—and still call itself Swedish?" Similarly by what right does a U.S. firm, or a Dutch firm, or a British firm maintain its national character, while deepening its involvement in foreign markets?

The Futures of Sweden study is thus significant in that it suggests that one small nation in seeking to maintain its way of life in a world society may have to be transformed by that world society.

Consider these new questions:

1. If Sweden's key institutions must invent a future in a global industrial system, what roles shall Sweden seek, suited to Swedish national character, aspirations and values? If Sweden will be, however unwillingly, globalized can she also in some measure, "Swedicize" the global industrial system?

2. The more Swedish multinationals are transformed into more truly multinational institutions, the more other institutions must be transformed, such as, for example, her educational system. How "blue and yellow" can Sweden stay? What is the alternative to being "blue and yellow?" A Swedish business leader put the question, "Sweden's values I understand and believe in. But *global* values—what are they? What can they ever be?"

Perhaps the key question should be: How can a small state protect what it believes in, socially, politically, culturally, while seeking a *leading* role in a global industrial system?

The fascinating and well-executed study of Lars Otterbeck and Gunnar Hedlund needs no further justification. By virtue of my respect and affection for Sweden and its way, I wish to add a Postscript to this significant study, and a Prologue to future studies.

POSTSCRIPT

The Global Futures Methodology

The "Futures of Sweden" study has unique features to suit the unique questions raised. It focuses on interviews with *persons* in key positions in trade unions, governments, and multinational firms, who respond to scenarios of various kinds of worlds. It can be contrasted with studies which are presented on statistical data on the world system, such as the Club of Rome.[1] By focusing on the Swedish concepts of a global future, we can begin to understand the seeds of the Swedish global future in the present.

Since the Futures of Sweden study is *comparative*, we can contrast how persons in small and say, large countries respond to similar global scenarios.

The Swedish institutional actors, firms, trade unions, government as *learning systems*, are trying to adapt simultaneously to new and changing national, regional, and global environments. This means that at various levels of policy, Sweden must be Swedish, Scandinavian, European, Western, transideological, LDC (Less Developed Countries) oriented, and global. We see that Swedish concepts of neutrality and morality cannot be applied without extensive interpenetration by the wishes and aspirations of other peoples, be they foreign workers, or foreign employees.

The MNC's pursuit of growth and profits everywhere, the trade union's primary concern with Swedish employment and welfare and the government's concern with various Swedish constituencies, including Swedish labor and business are abiding differences between these institutions. But the relatively rapid interaction between Swedish institutions could produce a kind of MNC schizophrenia. The Swedish MNC remains a leading economic system in Sweden because it acknowledges world markets and it uses financial resources and personnel outside the home country but it fears acting "too multinational." The rule may become: "Pretend you are Swedish, when you are in Sweden—but adapt everywhere in the world." Labor and government in Sweden must to some degree lag behind the rate of multinationalization of its firms. Paradoxically, the MNC for profit no doubt, accepts more of humanity as humans than do nationalistic nation states!

The study was designed to encourage a comparison of the kind of global consciousness of the Swedish leaders with leadership in other countries.

Comparative Findings—Sweden vs. USA.

A comparison with our research in the U.S. shows:

1. The Swedish leadership as a group accept a global future orientation

more than the U.S. leadership. But MNC's in both countries have global views more similar to each other than other institutions in the two countries.[2]

2. The Swedish leadership on the whole accepts dependence on the global industrial system more readily than the U.S. leaderhsip in trade unions and government. U.S. MNC's accept, however, their global destiny.

3. The Swedish trade unions seem to have more information about the character of global economic processes than the U.S. trade union leaders who are more preoccupied with internal problems.

4. The Swedish trade union leadership is seen to be in a coalition with the Swedish government, which has a defensive attitude towards the expansion of MNC's. They want influence on MNC's on what is recognized to be a largely irreversible phenomenon.

In the U.S. trade unions view the government and business in collusion. U.S. trade unions would like to bring U.S. business home!

The U.S. trade union leaders have a preference for an Ethnocentric-Restrictive scenario. They do not believe that dysfunctional consequences will result. The Swedish trade unions do not view the same scenario as desirable—at the top. At the grassroots, the matter may be different.

5. It is perhaps harder for the U.S. as a superpower to accept dependence on a global industrial system. Witness recent U.S. policies designed to reduce drastically U.S. dependence on Middle Eastern oil. Most experts consider these objectives unrealistic. But some U.S. leaders seem to need, at this juncture, to nourish the belief that entangling alliances—in the economic sphere—must be reduced over the long term. Swedes appear to accept that such a choice does not exist.

6. If there is a contrast between Swedish and U.S. MNE's it is that U.S. multinationals appear to accept that their character will be transformed over time, as they become more deeply dependent on foreign production. In the current political climate, it is perhaps understandable that in Sweden one would prefer not to be called "multinational" but international and hence remain de facto Swedish. U.S. MNC's may still believe that as they are geocentrized they will stay American. Some may have, privately, more confidence that they can Americanize the foreigners, as compared to Swedish firms. But multinationalism is becoming a more acceptable ideology in U.S. MNC's.

The readiness of Swedish leadership to accept as desirable and possible a Global Regulatory System is perhaps the most significant finding in the Futures of Sweden study. In the U.S. study the global regulatory and supportive scenario was combined in one scenario. Some U.S. executives preferred to see the supportive parts (with its laissez-faire aspect) rather than a global regulatory-framework (which appeared less realistic, when the U.S. study was started two years ago). But some U.S. executives were accepting of it in the longer term. The nature and form of the global regulatory framework U.S. MNC's probably accept as Swedes go, to the degree that the ethnocentric-restrictive world is too costly and the laissez-faire world unlikely.

U.S. trade union leaders found it difficult to speculate about a Global Regulatory scenario. They seemed to know little about international activities of U.S. firms. U.S. multinational's activities were primarily motivated, they felt, to get cheap labor. They would more likely prefer that U.S. government control U.S. firms everywhere in the world. Indeed as foreign investment in the U.S. increases, even with the promise of higher employment, we should expect U.S. trade unions to remain suspicious of the U.S. multinational.

Swedish trade unions leaders at the top are unique in their internationalism, and in their acceptance of the evolution of the trade union in a global industrial system. But if unemployment should rise markedly in Sweden, would there be a shift in this view?

The basic difference between the U.S. and Sweden is that, comparatively speaking, the feedback system between the key actors seems *not* to be working as well in the U.S. Suspicion of conspiratorial activities of U.S. firms to leave the U.S. is more characteristic of U.S. unions. There is little dialogue between U.S. unions and U.S. MNC's. The feedback system in Sweden by comparison works well at the top. U.S. trade unions and perhaps most U.S. legislators are *mystified* by U.S. multinationals and their global logic.

We asked U.S. executives to imagine a world where the U.S. is attacking its multinationals and Europe is welcoming multinationals as legitimate and desirable business institutions. This scenario is not too far fetched. It is implied in a work conducted for the French government by The Wharton School, suggesting that Paris become a global city welcoming multinationals by the year 2000.[3]

In such a world fully one third of the U.S. executives would consider locating their headquarters outside of the U.S. When such findings are known by politicians and trade union leaders, their beliefs that multinationals are inherently disloyal will be confirmed. U.S. trade unions have not yet recognized that for the most multinational of MNC's to change national character is easier than a catastrophic retreat from world markets. For at the heart of one trade union fantasy is that someday the multinationals will come home—in a more autarkic world to come!

A Global Systems Interpretation

We are but a step along a path to understanding how our global industrial system and global political system interact, influence, and transform each other. Processes as vast and complex as these are very difficult to see and understand at the national level. Similar studies must be conducted in other advanced, developing and socialist countries.

The evidence from this study and elsewhere is that, within the next decade, both MNC's and nation states will come to recognize that:

1. For advanced countries, an ethnocentric-restrictive world is either not workable or damaging to political and economic institutions. Even though the global industrial system is not under direct control by the fragmented global political system, two defensive options may have negative consequences.

A. The first defensive option is for each nation to try to contract or reverse the growth of multinational enterprises. The risk of a global recession appears likely to most Swedes and to some Americans.

B. The second defensive option is for home countries to attempt to control extraterritorially their home based multinationals. Such efforts to control would not be appreciated in host countries, to the degree that they are unilaterally applied. But the U.S. will be more reluctant to give up extraterritorial application of its laws, compared to Sweden.

The ethnocentric reflex of nations will be recognized over time as *counter-effective*. To the degree that this is widely accepted, this constitutes a kind of *learning* for a nation state.

2. At the same time a global laissez-faire scenario, in an era of increasing exposure and concern with multinationals could not gain wide acceptance. While the multinationals could thrive in such a climate (they believe), world opinion seems to be growing that letting MNC's function in a "constraint free" world does not fit the values and beliefs of the latter third of the twentieth century. Stakeholders like consumers, competitors, trade unions, government want to influence the MNC.

Only some leaders in the U.S. administration still advocate a 19th century liberal laissez-faire attitude toward multinationals. U.S. MNE's will recognize that the world has changed.

3. The third alternative, the global regulatory world accepted as most desirable by Swedes contains some major dilemmas.

However desirable intergovernmental multilateral agreements may be, they are hard to come by, on the world scale—if we include the Less Developed Countries and the socialist countries of Eastern Europe.

But if a global regulatory world is a precondition for a viable and legitimate MNC a common core of global values regarding the actual and potential contribution of the MNC must be held widely. What are these values?

MNC's are sensitive about codes, and guidelines, terms which imply MNC's are "bad" citizens. Executives envision U.N. bureaucracies wallowing in mountains of data—trying to limit the MNC freedom to make complex marketing, financial and production decisions.

MNE's may already want to admit that eventually the global political system must be preceived to contain and control the global industrial system—but they want to maintain the MNC's vitality and entrepreneurial character.

So where will the guidelines come from—guidelines which will be seen as fair and enforceable—by all the interested parties?

PROLOGUE TO FUTURE RESEARCH

What of future research on the nation state in the global industrial system? In my view, the search is underway for a *Global Value System* which regulates MNC's but binds nation states (and also by definition limits their sovereignty). Commonly held ideas about what good MNC's should do in all countries are being articulated. Global regulatory scenarios may begin at a regional level, say the EEC. But if guidelines are to succeed they must be perceived by nation states and MNC's as desirable, feasible, and subject to rewards for compliance and penalties for noncompliance. And they must be flexible. A most difficult task!

It is instructive to look at the recent United Nations report for some clues. Although the norms and values emerging are oriented to a rich-poor country dichotomy, they are aimed at a wider audience and hence deserve attention.

An emergent global value system regarding MNC's
Consider these recommendations by the U.N. Committee on multinational corporations.[4]

In the Area of Technology, the U.N. Group recommended that:
1. "Before a multinational corporation is permitted to introduce a particular product into the domestic market, the host government should carefully evaluate its *suitability for meeting local needs.*"
2. "*A world patents (technology) bank be established* to which any public institution may donate for use in developing countries patents which it owns or purchases."
3. "Home countries do not hamper the process of transfer by multinational corporations of the *production of labor-intensive* and *low skill* products to *developing countries,* and that they protect the domestic work force displaced by this transfer, through adjustment assistance measures such as retraining and re-employment in more productive and higher paying jobs, and not through restrictions on imports."
4. "The *international standards of disclosure,* accounting and reporting should include data which are of special relevance for the purpose of collective bargaining."

In the Consumer Protection Area:
5. "Home countries should *publicize prohibitions and restrictions* on products, or ingredients of products, found to be hazardous to health, and should consider whether their export should also be prohibited or made conditional upon specific approval by the importing country."

This random selection of recommendations points up emergent values (some are already accepted) and also emergent conflicts.

Emergent Value 1: Host government developing criteria for local adaptation of products, screening product suitability in terms of economic, social and cultural priorities of the nation states.

Emergent Value 2: Geocentric technology by increasing the full use of technology, globally, especially to LDCs.

Emergent Value 3: Transfer of production to LDC's by the free transfer of labor intensive work to lesser developed countries.

Emergent Value 4: International accounting standards, the development of international rules for reporting MNC activities.

Emergent Value 5: Protectring the consumer worldwide.

Conflicts are likely, of course. On the one hand, home countries are urged in some areas *not to interfere* with the beneficial effects MNE's can have on host countries. On the other, home countries are asked to *inhibit* negative impacts of their MNC's on host countries. Helping LDC's even at the expense of the home country (*see* No. 3) is not yet an accepted value.

What is of central importance is that an emerging, if fragile, belief *that home and host countries MNC's, and trade unions must coordinate to find new norms acceptable to all parties and conforming to standards of international economic justice.*

In a world complicated by national differences, and rivalries—political, economic, and military—nourishing that global value will be no mean achievement!

Obstacles

There are other powerful obstacles to a global regulatory scenario:

1. There can be no international regulatory agency because there is no international government.

2. There are wide divergences between the left and the right regarding the MNCs.

On the left, the MNC is seen as imperialistic, taking over the global political system through a tight control of the global industrial system.

On the right, the MNC is seen as a sign of economic growth, profit seeking to be sure, but a source of wealth nonetheless.

The MNC is treated as a loosely linked fragmented system reflecting the world's political organization. A new and more persuasive orientation is a total systems approach to the MNC and its impacts on many nation states. For this approach, the values inherent in the ethnocentric scenario seem least suitable.

Universal codes, controls, guidelines, need inputs from all countries.

For a country like Sweden, the choice may be one of either being inactive regarding the emergence of global values regarding MNC's or else working with other nations to build an equitable framework within which its key institutions of the future, including the Swedish MNC, must live.

CONCLUSION

In his *History of Sweden*,[5] Ingvar Andersson, notes the profound changes that the last thirty years have produced.

Agriculture, forestry, and fishing which in 1940 employed close to 30 percent of the population now are less than 8 percent, while the percentage of those employed in industry and public services rises.

He concludes his work with this statement:

"The last few generations have thus seen the old peasant country transformed into an industrial nation, the many small villages superseded by thriving towns, the distinctive dialects replaced by a more uniform spoken language under the influence of schools, radio and television: they have also seen land cultivated since the stone age change character, in common with the wilds. This changing Sweden faces the future with confidence." (p. 465).

What of a future in the global industrial system? Torgny Segerstedt conjectures about this future with less optimism:

"In 1985 Sweden will not be able to isolate herself in any area of life. Industry, trade, environmental protection, research, leisure and politics will be internationally oriented. Because of this, her national decisions, her autonomy and sovereignty will be undermined . . ." (p. 155).[6]

"The important questions for the small industrial countries will certainly be the relationship between the domestic and multinational industries. The decisive question is if the latter will become really international or merely the expression of industrial imperialism, which would mean that their real management will have its headquarters in one or the other big power states and hence that the small countries will be unable to influence events." (P. 163).

But if multinational enterprises become truly multinational, ownership, top management, and the cities in which they are located must become more multinational. So must universities. How multinational can Sweden become in order to avoid being a place for subsidiaries and not headquarters?

There are more small nations than super powers. Their challenge—now global in character—is to influence the design of the global regulatory scenario, to recall that the global industrial system still can be shaped by national values, National pride and belief in some cultural values are a protection against the fears of indentity loss that emerging global values may produce.

But the next generations of Sweden, the future history of Sweden may depend more on accepting that all Swedes are part of the continous, splendid and multicultured fabric of humanity in the global age to come. Small nations may find it easier to understand their inherent limitations in resources, their obligations to develop a pluralistic world, with internationalism in its key institutions as a strength, not a weakness.

In such a world, the big nations, like the U.S., in some heroic insight may look to the smaller nations as models for the future.

NOTES

1. Dennis Meadows, *et al., The Limits to Growth,* N.Y.: University Books, 1972.
2. A book written with my colleagues Franklin Root and Bernard Mennis is being prepared focusing on the findings in the U.S.
3. *Paris: Viile Internationale, Roles et Vocation,* Travaux et Recherches de Prospective Schema General d'Amenagement de la France: Datar, No. 39, La Documentation Française.
4. "The Impact of Multinational Corporation on the Development Process and On International Relations," Report of the group of eminent persons to study the role of multinational corporations on development and on international relations, The Economic and Social Affairs Council of the United Nations, E/5500/Add. 1 (Part I), May 24, 1974.
5. Ingvar Andersson, *A History of Sweden,* Stockholm: Natur och Kultur, 1970.
6. T. Segerstedt, "The Smaller Nation in the International Marketplace," *The Future of the Corporation,* H. Kahn (ed.), N.Y.: Mason and Lipscomb, 1974.

BIBLIOGRAPHY

Ackoff, R. L. Scientific Method. N.Y.: John Wiley and Sons, 1962.

—————. A Concept of Corporate Planning. N.Y.: John Wiley and Sons, 1970.

—————. "Background of a City's Foreground." France: Breau sans Nappe, mimeographed, 1972.

Ackoff, R. L. and F. E. Emery. On Purposeful Systems. Chicago, Ill.: Aldine Press, 1972.

Ackoff, R. L. Redesigning the Future. N.Y.: John Wiley and Sons, 1974.

AFL-CIO. The Impact of U.S. Foreign Direct Investment on U.S. Employment and Trade: An Assessment of Critical Claims and Legislative Proposals. Washington, D.C.: AFL-CIO, 1971.

Anderson, I. A History of Sweden. Stockholm: Natur och Kultur, 1970.

Angyal, A. Foundations for a Science of Personality. Cambridge, Mass.: Harvard University Press, 1941.

Annerstedt, J. and L. Dencik. "Koloniseringen av Framtiden" ("The Colonization of the Future"). Ord och Bild. Volume 6, 1971.

Behrman, J. N. U.S. International Business and Governments. N.Y.: McGraw-Hill, 1971.

—————. National Interests and the Multinational Enterprise: Tensions Among the North Atlantic Countries. Englewood Cliffs, N.J.: Prentice-Hall, 1970.

Bell, D. (ed.). Toward the Year 2000. Boston, Mass.: Beacon Press, 1969.

Blake, D. H. "Trade Unions and the Challenge of Multinational Corporations." The Annals of the American Academy of Political and Social Sciences. September, 1972.

Blalock, H.M. Causal Inferences in Nonexperimental Research. Chapel Hill, N.C.: University of North Carolina Press, 1964.

Bludhorn, C. G. "A Case for American Nationalism." Business Week. (September), 1973.

Bornschier, V. "Multinationale Wirtschaftskroporationen—Eine Form Organisationeller Uberschichtung im Weltmass-stab" ("The MNC—A Form of Organizational Overlayer in the World System"). Zurich: Universitat Zurich, mimeographed (December), 1973.

—————. "Der Einfluss der Grosse von Industrielandern auf die Multinationalisierung ihrer Wirstchaftsunternehmen" ("The Influence of the Size of Industrial Countries on the Multinationalization of Their Corporations"). Zurich: Zurich: Sociologisches Institut der Universitat Zurich. December, mimeographed, 1973.

Bradley, G. E. and E. C. Bursk. "Multinationalism and the 29th Day." Harvard Business Review. January/February, 1972.

Brooke, M. Z. and H. Remmers. The Strategy of Multinational Enterprise. N.Y.: American Elsevier, 1970.

Buckley, W. Sociology and Modern Systems Theory. Englewood Cliffs, N.J.: Prentice Hall, 1967.

Burenstam, Linder S. An Essay on Trade and Transformation. Stockholm: Almqvist and Widsell, 1961.

Burtis, D., F. Lavipour, S. Ricciardi and K. P. Sauvant (eds). Multinational Corporation—Nation-State Interaction, An Annotated Bibliography. Philadelphia, Pa.: Foreign Policy Research Institute, 1971.

Chevalier, M. A Wider Range of Perspectives in the Bureaucratic Structure. Ottawa: The Royal Commission on Bilingualism and Biculturalism, 1966.

—————. Stimulation of Needed Social Science Research for Canadian Water Resource Problems. Ottawa: Privy Council Science Secretariat, 1967.

—————. "Interest Group Planning." Philadelphia, Pa.: University of Pennsylvania, mimeographed, 1968.

————— and R. T. Taylor. "Dynamics of Adoption in the Federal Public Service." Ottawa: The Royal Commission on Bilingualism and Biculturalism, mimeographed, 1971.

Churchman, C. W. *The Systems Approach.* N.Y.: Delta Books, 1968.

Cooper, R. N. "Trade Policy is Foreign Policy." *Economic Impact.* Volume 13, 1.73.

Docherty, P. *Organisationsutvecking for Okat Medinflytande i Tjanstemanna-foretag.* Stockholm: EFI, Delrapport 6, Forskarroller i ett Aktionsforsking-sprojekt (Report 6, Researcher Roles in an Action Research Project), 1976.

Dreze, J. "Quelques Reflexions Sereines sur l'Adaptation de l'Industrie Belge au Marche Commun" ("Some Serious Reflections on the Adaptation of Belgian Industry to the Common Market"). *Unpublished mimeograph,* 1976.

—————. "Lex Exportations Intra-C.E.E. en 1958 et la Position Belge." *Recherches Economiques de Lovain.* Volume 8, 1961.

Dunning, J. H. *Studies in International Investment.* London: George Allen and Urwin, Ltd., 1970.

Dymsza, W. A. *Multinational Business Strategy.* N.Y.: McGraw-Hill, 1972.

Eliasson, G. *International Competitiveness: An Empirical Analysis of Swedish Manufacturing.* Stockholm: Industriforbundet, 1972.

—————. *Diagnos pa 70-Talet (Diagnosis in the 70s).* Stockholm: Industriforbundet, 1971.

Emery, F. E. (ed.). *Systems Thinking.* London: Penguin Press, 1969.

—————. "The Next Thirty Years: Concepts, Methods and Anticipations." *Human Relations.* Volume 20, 1967.

—————. "Futures We're In." Canberra: Australian National University, Centre for Continuing Education, *mimeographed,* 1974.

—————. and E. L. Trist. *Towards a Social Ecology: Contextual Apprecia-tions of the Future in the Present.* London and N.Y.: Plenum Press, 1973.

—————. "The Causal Texture of Organizational Environments." *Human Relations.* 18:21-32, 1965.

Engman, H. *Foretagens Internationalistering—Valfardshot eller Framstegs-garanti? (The Internationalization of Corporations—Threat to Welfare or Guarantee of Progress?).* Lund: Prisma, 1973.

—————. *Sverige och Europa (Sweden and Europe).* Stockholm: Prisma and TCO, 1973.

Fayerweather, J. *International Business Management: A Conceptual Framework.* N.Y.: McGraw-Hill, 1969.

Foreign Privy Council. *Foreign Ownership and the Structure of Canadian Industry.* Ottawa: Foreign Privy Council, 1968.

Forsyth, D. "Foreign-owned Firms and Labor Relations—A Regional Perspective." *British Journal of Industrial Relations.* March, 1973.

Franko, L. B. "Strategic Planning for Internationalization: The European Dilemma and Some Possible Solutions." *Long Range Planning,* June, 1973.

—————. "The Growth, Organizational Structure and Allocative Efficiency of European Multinational Firms: Some Emerging Hypotheses." Geneva: Centre d'Etudes Industrielles, *mimeographed,* 1972.

—————. *European Business Strategies in the United States.* Geneva: Business International, 1971.

Georgescu-Roegen, N. *The Entropy Law and the Economic Process.* Cambridge, Mass.: Harvard University Press, 1971.

Goldfinger, N. "The Case for Burke-Hartke." *Columbia Journal of World Business.* Volume 13 (Spring), 1973.

Gross, B. M. (ed.). *Action Under Planning.* N.Y.: McGraw-Hill, 1966.

Harbison, F. and C. A. Myers. *Management in the Industrial World.* N.Y.: McGraw-Hill, 1959.

Harre, R. and P. F. Secord. *The Explanation of Social Behavior.* Oxford: Oh.: Basil Blackwell, 1972.

Haynes, E. "A Challenge to the Critics of U.S. Foreign Investment." *Columbia Journal of World Business.* 13 (Spring), 1973.

Hedlund, G. "De Multinationella Foretagens Framtid" ("The Future of the Multinational Corporations"). In J. E. Vahlne (ed), *Foretagsekonomisk Forskning om Internationellt Foretagande (Business Economic Rese-arch on International Enterprising).* Stockholm: Norstedts, 1974.

————— (ed.). "Futures of Sweden in a Global Industrial System." Report from a seminar at the Swedish Institute of Management, Yxtaholm, 1973.

Hirsch, S. *Location of Industry and International Competitiveness.* Oxford, Oh.: Claredon Press, 1967.

Huntford, R. *The New Totalitarians.* London: The Penguin Press, 1971.

ICC. *Guidelines for International Investment.* Paris: International Chamber of Commerce. No. 272, 1972.

ICC. *Realities-Multinational Enterprises Respond on Basic Issues.* Stockholm: International Chamber of Commerce, 1974.

ILO Multinational Enterprises and Social Police. Geneva: ILO, 1973.

Department of Industry. "Tillsattandet av Arbetsgrupp med Uppgift att Folja Fragor Rorande Multinationella Foretag." Industridepartmentet. ("Insitution of Work Group to Followup on Questions Concerning Multinational Corporations," extract from Department of Industry's minutes, 03-22.), 1973.

Department of Industry. *Multinational Corporations.* Stockholm: Department of Industry, 1973.

INTERPLAN. *Appraising Administrative Capabilities for Development.* A methodological monograph prepared by the International Group Studies in National Planning (INTERPLAN). N.Y.: United Nations, 1969.

"Internationell Facklig Overskit Samarbetet Over Granserna Okar" ("International Trade Union Survey: Cooperation Across Borders is Increasing"). *Arbetsgivaren,* August 9, 1972.

James, J. A. "Multinational Trade Unions Muscle Their Strength." *European Business.* Autumn, 1973.

Jantsch, E. *Technological Planning and Social Futures.* London: Cassell and Company, Ltd., 1972.

—————. "The World Corporation: The Total Committment." *Columbia Journal of World Business.* May-June, 1971.

—————. *Technological Forecasting in Perspective.* Paris: OECD, 1966.

Kahn, H. and A. J. Wiener. *The Year 2000: A Framework for Speculation.* London: McMillan, 1967.

Keegan, W. J. *Multinational Marketing Management.* Homewood, Ill.: Irwin, 1974.

Kindleberger, E. P. (ed.). *The International Corporation.* Cambridge, Mass.: The MIT Press, 1970.

—————. *American Business Abroad: Six Lectures on Direct Investment.* New Haven, Conn.: Yale University Press, 1969.

Knickerbocker, R. T. *Oligopolistic Reactions and Multinational Enterprise.* Cambridge, Mass.: Harvard University Press, 1973.

Kohler, W. "Physical Gestalten." In W. D. Ellis (ed.), *A Source Book of Gestalt Psychology.* N.Y.: Harcourt, Brace and World, 1938.

Kristensson, F. and H. Engman. "Det Multinationella Foretaget, Fackforeningen och Nationalstaten" ("The Multinational Enterprise, the Trade Union and the Nation State"). *Internationalla Studier.* Volume 2, 1973.

Levinson, C. *De Multionella Foretagen och Inflationen (Multinational Corporations and Inflation).* London: Allen and Unwin, 1972.

—————. *Fackforeningsrorelsen och de Multinationalla Foretagen (Trade Unionism and Multinational Corporations).* Utrikespolitiska Institutetet, Varldspolitikens Dagsfragor 12, 1972.

—————. *International Trade Unionism.* London: George Allen and Unwin, 1972.

————— and P. Sanden. *Kapitalets International (The International of Capital).* Stockholm: Prisma, 1972.

Lewin, K. *Topological Psychology.* N.Y.: McGraw-Hill, 1936.

Lindberg, L. N. "Some Things About Long-Term Planning that Worry Me." France: Breau sans Nappe, *mimeographed* (October), 1972.

—————. "A Prospectus of Political Futures: The Theory and Practice of Post-Industrial Society." Madison, Wisc.: University of Wisconsin, *mimeographed,* 1972.

Lindqvist, S. "Utsugning eller u-Hjalp" ("Exploitation or Development Aid"). *Kommentar.* Volume 2, 1970.

LO. "Multinationella Foretag och Fackligt Internationellt Arbeite" ("Multinational Corporations and International Trade Unionism"). Stockholm: Motions No. 345-355 at the June 1971 National Conference of LO, 1971.

Luchins, A. S. and E. H. Luchins. *Logical Foundations of Mathematics for Behavioral Scientists.* N.Y.: Holt, Rinehart and Winston, 1965.

Lund, H. *Svenska Foretagsinvesteringar i Utlandet. (Swedish Investment Abroad).* Stockholm: Industrifordundets Forlat, 1967.

Macrae, N. "The Future of International Business." *The Economist.* January (Special supplement), 1972.

Mandel, E. *EEC och Konkurrensen Europa—USA (EEC and the Competition Europe—USA).* Halmstad: Lilla Partisanserien, 1969.

Meadows, D. H., D. L. Meadows, J. Randers and W. W. Behrens, III. *The Limits to Growth.* N.Y.: Universe Books, 1972.

"Multinationals: A Step Towards Global Bargaining." *Business Week.* Volume 28, 1972.

Myrdal, H. G. "LO's lonepolitik och Mr. Levinson" (Lo's Wage Policy and Mr. Levinson"). *Svenska Dagbladet* (Newspaper). April, 1974.

Olsson, J. "Internationella Fragor—Multinationella Foretag" ("International Issues—Multinational Corporations"). Stockholm: LO, 1972.

Otterbeck, Lars. "International Foretagslokalisering och Multinationella Foretag" ("International Location of Industry and Multinational Corporations"). *Skandivaiska Enskilda Bankens Kvartalsskrift.* 3:86-94, 1973

—————. "Ultalandsberoendet i Svensk Industri" ("Foreign Dependency in Swedish Industry"). *Ekonomen.* 11:24-26, 1973.

Ozbekham, H. "Towards A General Theory of Planning." In E. Jantisch (ed.), *Perspectives of Planning.* Paris: OECD, 1969.

—————. "Thoughts on the Emerging Methodology of Planning." Philadelphia, Pa.: University of Pennsylvania, Social Systems Science Department, *mimeographed,* 1973.

"Travaux et Recherches de Prospective Schema General d'Amenagement de la France." Paris: Ville Internationale, Roles et Vocation. *Datar No. 39,* La Documentation Francaise.

Perlmutter, H. V. "The Multinational Enterprise in Decade One of the Emerging Global Industrial System." Philadelphia, Pa.: Multinational Enterprise Unite, *mimeographed,* 1973.

—————. "The Multinational Firm and the Future." *The Annals of the American Academy of Political and Social Science.* September, 1972.

—————. "Super-Giant Firms of the Future." *Wharton Quarterly.* Volume 3 (Winter), 1968.

—————. "L'enterprise Internationale—Trois Conceptions." *Revue Economique et Sociale.* Volume 23 (May), 1965.

—————, F. R. Root and L. Plante. "Responses of U.S.-based MNCs to Alternative Public Policy Futures." *Columbia Journal of World Business.* XIII(3) (Fall), 1973.

Pisar, S. "Nationalism and the Multinational Corporation." *Dialogue, Volume 2, 1973.*

Popper, K. R. *The Poverty of Historicism.* N.Y.: Harper and Row, 1961.

Quinn, J. B. "Technology Transfer by Multinational Companies." *Harvard Business Review.* November/December, 1969.

"Rapport om de Multinationella Foretagen" ("Report on Multinational Corporations"). *Svenska Metallindustriarbetarforbundet,* 1973.

Roberts, B. C. "Multinational Collective Bargaining—A European Perspective?" *British Journal of Industrial Relations.* March, 1973.

Robock, S. and K. Simmonds. *International Business and Multinational Enterprises.* Homewood, Ill.: Irwin, 1973.

Root, F. R. "Interdependence and Adaption: Response Patterns of U.S.-based MNCs to Restrictive and Supportive Public Policy Worlds." Philadelphia, Pa.: University of Pennsylvania, Worldwide Institutions Group, *mimeographed,* 1974.

Ruttenberg, S. H. *Needed: A Constructive Foreign Trade Policy.* Washington, D.C.: AFL-CIO, 1971.

Sampson, A. *Varldsmakten ITT (The Soverign State of ITT)*. N.Y.: Stein and Day, 1973.

Schollhammer, H. "Strategies and Methodologies in International Business and Comparative Management." *Management International Review*. Volume 13, 1973.

Schon, D. A. *Beyond the Stable State*. N.Y.: Random House, 1971.

Segerstedt, T. "The Smaller Nation in the International Marketplace." In H. Kahn (ed.), *The Future of the Corporation*. N.Y.: Mason and Lipscomb, 1974.

Selznick, P. *Leadership in Administration*. Evanston, Ill.: Row Peterson, 1957.

Sethi, S. P. and J. N. Sheth (eds.). *Multinational Business Operations*. Five Volumes. Pacific Palisades, Cal.: Goodyear Publishing Company, 1973.

Shonfield, A. *Modern Capitalism*. London: Oxford University Press, 1966.

SIY, "Att Valja Framtic" ("To Choose a Future"). *Statens Offentliga Utredningar*. Volume 59, 1972.

Stobaugh, R. B., *et al.* "U.S. Multinational Enterprises and the U.S. Economy." Boston, Mass.: Harvard Business School, *mimeographed,* 1972.

Stopford, J. M. *Growth and Organization Change in the Multinational Firm*. Cambridge, Mass.: Harvard University Press, 1968.

"Sveriges 1,000 Storsta Foretag 1972" ("The 1,000 Largest Companies in Sweden in 1972"). Stockholm: A Table in *Veckans Affarer,* 1973.

Sveriges Industriforbund. *De Multinationella i Sverige (Multinationals in Sweden)*. Stockholm: Sveriges Industriforbund, 1973.

Swedenborg, B. *Den Svenska Industrins Investeringar i Utlandet (Swedish Industry's Investments Abroad)*. Uppsala: Industriens Utrednings, 1973.

Sweden—Towards a Post-Industrial Society. Geneva: *Business International,* 1971.

TCO och det Internationella Fackliga Samarbetet (TCO and International Trade Cooperation). TCO, 1973.

Thomas, I. M. and W. G. Bennis. *The Management of Change and Conflict*. London: Penguin Books, 1972.

Toffler, A. *Future Shock*. London: Bodley Head, 1970.

Trist, E. L. "Organisation et Systeme: Quelques Remarques theoriques se rapportant plus particullerement aux recherches d'Andras Angyal" ("Organization and Systems: Some Theoretical Research on Particularly the Research of Andras Angyal"). *Revue Francaise de Sociologie*. Volumes 11-12, 1970-1971.

Tungendhat, C. *De Multinationella (The Multinationals)*. Stockholm: Prisma, 1972.

Turner, L. *Storforetagen tar Makten (The Power of Multinational Enterprising)*. Stockholm: Wahlstrom and Widstrand, 1974.

U.N. *The Impact of Multinational Corporations on the Development Process and on International Relations*. N.Y.: The Economic and Social Affairs Council of the United Nations. E/5500/Add 1, Part 1, 1974.

U.N. *Multinational Corporations in World Development*. N.Y.: The Economic and Social Affairs Council of the United Nations, 1973.

"The Unions Get the Ear in Brussels." *Vision*. June, 1973.

Vahlne, J. E. (ed.). *Foretagsekonomisk Forskning om Internationellt Foretagande (Business Economic Research on International Enterprising)*. Stockholm: Norstedts, 1974.

Vernon, R. *Sovereignty at Bay: The Multinational Spread of U.S. Enterprises*. N.Y.: Basic Books, 1971.

—————. *The Economic and Political Consequences of Multinational Enterprise:* An Anthology. Cambridge, Mass.: Harvard University Press, 1972.

————— (ed.). *The Technology Factor in International Trade*. N.Y.: National Bureau of Economic Research, 1970.

Vickers, Sir G. *The Art of Judgement*. London: Chapman and Hall, 1966.

Wells, L. T. (ed.). *The Product Life Cycle and International Trade*. Cambridge, Mass.: Harvard University Press, 1972.

Wertheimer, M. "The General Theoretical Situation." In W. D. Ellis (ed.), *A Source Book of Gestalt Psychology*. N.Y.: Harcourt Brace and World, 1974.

Wikstrom, S. and I. Kord. "Omvarldsprognoser och Tekniker" ("Techniques for Environmental Forecasts"). Stockholm: University of Stockholm, *mimeographed,* 1974.

Wohlin, L., *et al. Svensk Industri 1972-1977 (Swedish Industry 1972-1977).* Stockholm: Industriesn Utredningsinstitut, 1973.